Where One Is Gathered in His Name

Where One Is Gathered in His Name

DAN R. CRAWFORD

BROADMAN PRESS
Nashville, Tennessee

Unless otherwise indicated, Scripture quotations are from the *New American Standard Bible.* Copyright © The Lockman Foundation, 1960, 1962, 1963, 1968, 1971, 1972, 1973, 1975, 1977. Used by permission. Those marked (KJV) are from the King James Version of the Bible. Those marked (NIV) are from the HOLY BIBLE *New International Version,* copyright © 1978, New York Bible Society. Used by permission. Those marked (TLB) are from *The Living Bible.* Copyright © Tyndale House Publishers, Wheaton, Illinois, 1971. Used by permission.

Dewey Decimal Classification: 242.2
Subject Headings: DEVOTIONS, DAILY // SINGLE PEOPLE
Library of Congress Catalog Card Number: 85-19519
Printed in the United States of America

Library of Congress Cataloging-in-Publication Data

Crawford, Dan R., 1941-
    Where one is gathered in His name.

    Includes index.
    1. Spiritual exercises.   I. Title.
BV4832.2.C72 1986   248.3   85-19519
ISBN 0-8054-5025-4

Some of the materials in this book were first published in a Doctor of Ministry project written by the author at Southwestern Baptist Theological Seminary, Fort Worth, Texas, under the title, *Developing a Program of Private Worship for Student Short-Term Missionaries* © 1981. Used by permission.

Some of the materials in this book were published by the Home Mission Board, Southern Baptist Convention, written by the author under the title, *First Things First: Daily Guide for Summer Missionaries* © 1983. Used by permission.

To W. F. Howard, **ONE,** who modeled for me both the discipline of the daily quiet time with God and the life-style of Christian servanthood

and

To my brother, Bob, **ONE** of many single adults in my life who teaches me a fuller meaning of **ONE** . . . gathered in His name.

PREFACE

Why would anyone need a prescription like this? The doctor had just handed me my new prescription calling for one hundred pills to be taken once a day for the next one hundred days. When I inquired as to why, his response was, "You need the pill to help balance your health, and you need a hundred to get you in the habit of taking them."

Why would anyone need a book like this? To paraphrase my doctor, you need the daily activities to balance your spiritual health, and after one hundred days you ought to have formed a habit.

There are many balances needed in the Christian life. This book concerns itself with only the general balance between worship and service. Specifically, the book is concerned with the balance of private worship, where one is gathered in His name, and public service. The purpose of worship is not only personal fullness of the presence of God but unselfish service among the people of God. Thus, the book presents a challenge to individuals to find a working balance between their worship of God and their service among people.

Most Christians are familiar with the words of Jesus, "For where two or three have gathered together in My name, there I am in their midst" (Matt. 18:20). Jesus did not make that statement to exclude the value of one . . . gathered in His name. Rather, the statement was made to assure all of us of His presence, regardless of the number who have gathered. His own practice of being alone is enough proof of the importance of one . . . gathered in His name. Today's one may be a child, a teenager, a college student, a single adult, an adult married to a non-Christian, or it may well be one who is married to another Christian but who understands that we stand individually before God—singular in His presence. The important point is that singular servanthood is dependent on singular responsibility to God. While it is true that we draw strength from our association with other believers and together we accomplish much, it is also true that plural ability begins with singular servanthood.

More specifically, you are challenged to a hundred days of singular servanthood. You are challenged to a hundred days of reading *Bible-based thoughts* related to the Christian life. You are challenged to a hundred days of *reader's response* to the written material with your own thoughts. You are challenged to a hundred days of prayer, completing each day the *prayer to complete.* You are challenged to a hundred days of *going deeper* in study as you respond to the daily materials designed for such.

Having worked with and alongside many Christian servants, one clear observation is applicable to this book. The Christian servant has a tendency to lose the balance between worship and service. The purpose of this book is to challenge Christians to find a daily balance between their worship of God and their service among people. I hope it becomes habit-forming for you.

You may want to begin a notebook to do the exercises in this book. The amount of space allowed in the book may not be sufficient for your answers.

In the back of the book, you will find my acknowledgment of those who have helped me with this book. There is also a Scripture index to the entire book. Best wishes for a great 100 days.

Daily Guide to Singular Servanthood

I knelt and said,
"But I am one, only one."

And the world is so large. And evil is so strong. There are so few who
care. There are so few who sense.
"But I am one, only one."

The machines of organization roll on, crushing the individual into a part
of the mass. The hopelessness of the world-wrought minds spreads and
smothers the hope of the lonely individuals.
"But I am one, only one."

Entire cities have been destroyed. Entire nations have reaped their
seeds of distrust and lie writhing in their death throes.
"But I am one, only one."

While I eat my fill, hundreds die in hunger. While I close my door in
careless safety, hundreds watch doors in fear and resignation.
"But I am one, only one."

The powers of mind and thought and measurement reduce the world to
calculated probabilities.
"But I am one, only one."

And even that one walks in fear and stumbling, discontent, and lack of
strength.
"And I am so one, only one."

And he said,
"Stand up,
I choose you."

And I stood up and the earth trembled,
And that is the beginning to which there is no end,
Except in God.

DAY 1 ——————————————— DATE ——————————
The God Whom You Serve

"You shall have no other gods before Me (Ex. 20:3).

The one, supreme, personal God desires to have fellowship with people and to be worshiped by people. That is an overwhelming thought! Concerning other gods, the Lord says, "You shall not worship them or serve them; for I, the Lord your God, am a jealous God" (Ex. 20:5).

God desires that you have communion with Him, and this includes daily worship. "God is spirit; and those who worship Him must worship in spirit and truth" (John 4:24). As one worthy of worship, God took the initiative in creating humans for fellowship with Himself.

Likewise, God desires that you be on mission for Him, and this includes service. Mission service originated with God. Throughout the Bible, God's purpose is stated for "the nations" beginning in Genesis 9 with Noah and continuing to Revelation 7 when the nations gather around the throne in heaven.

As you serve God daily, you continue in a long line of servants. Paul called himself a servant (Gal. 1:10; 2 Cor. 3:6; Rom. 1:1) and indicated that Timothy was a servant (Phil. 1:1). Christ is described as a servant (Mark 10:45). Service and being on mission for God are interrelated. Service and witness on behalf of God are interrelated.

The God who made you and called you desires that you serve Him. That ought to be enough to get you started.
Reader's Response

A Prayer to Complete

God, You are so worthy of my praise and honor and service. May I be relatedly worthy of Your call. I acknowledge you today as . . .

Going Deeper

1. In Exodus 20:5-6 what will be the results of those who refuse to worship God? And of those who do worship Him?

2. List some characteristics of true worship as explained by Jesus in John 4:19-26.

   (1) _____

   (2) _____

   (3) _____

   (4) _____

   (5) _____

3. In what way is God's missionary purpose for "all nations" seen in the following verses?

   (1) John 12:32 _____

   (2) Matthew 13:37-38 _____

   (3) Matthew 28:19-20 _____

   (4) Acts 1:8 _____

4. In Mark's account of the conversation between Jesus and the brothers James and John, there is a great lesson related to service. See if you can find that lesson. (Mark 10:35-45).

5. What are two actions you could perform today that would be considered serving God?

   (1) _____

   (2) _____

DAY 2 ━━━━━━━━━━━━━━━ DATE _____

Missions in the Midst

"Go therefore and make disciples" (Matt. 28:19).

From the very beginning of His ministry, Jesus intended to share the gospel with all humankind. Scriptures such as Matthew 28:19-20; Mark 16:15-17; Luke 24:47-49; and Acts 1:6-8 give support to this idea. Jesus paved the way for worldwide missions as He consciously and with intent gave up His own life (Matt. 20:28), becoming the propitiation for the sins of all (1 John 2:2).

Because man was created "in the image of God" (Gen. 1:26-27), he is by nature filled with a deep longing for God. There is a vacuum in a person's life that can only be filled with the presence of God. According to the apostle Paul, human beings are sinful creatures who have fallen short of the "glory of God" (Rom. 3:23).

Since humanity is fallen and lost apart from a saving knowledge of Jesus Christ and since we know the full and meaningful life of a believer, it follows that we ought to share Jesus with all humankind.

There is in our day a necessity for each Christian to be a missionary both where he or she lives and in the total world. Christ's command obligates us to witness both where we live and "to the remotest part of the earth" (Acts 1:8), and God has chosen you (John 15:16) to "bear fruit" for Him on this day. May God bless you today as you experience missions in the midst of mankind.

Reader's Response

A Prayer to Complete

Father, as I go please make Your presence felt within me. I cannot go alone, but with You I can do all things. Help me today as I attempt to "bear fruit" in . . .

Going Deeper

1. Of what significance is it to missions that Jesus sent His disciples out in groups of two for a short term after which they were to give a report to Him (Luke 10:1-24)?

2. List three ways that you anticipate "being a missionary" in your field of service.

   (1) _____

   (2) _____

14

(3) _____

3. Jesus warned against "looking" away to the harvest and encouraged His disciples to begin immediately reaping the harvest (John 4:34-35). What are three ways you can be a missionary this week?

(1) _____
(2) _____
(3) _____

4. Meditate for a moment on the statement, "God has chosen you to 'bear fruit' for Him on this day." What does that statement mean to you?

DAY 3 ═══════════════ DATE _____

Meet Him in the Morning

"In the morning, O Lord, Thou wilt hear my voice;/In the morning I will order my prayer to Thee and eagerly watch" (Ps. 5:3).

The psalmist had learned what you must learn. Worship is essential to service. Your basic priority relationship is to God. One cannot share what one does not have; so, one's communication with God must remain open and active.

This communication will often be difficult, especially where self-discipline is weak. Your desire to serve God will often supersede your desire to worship God. The demands of the day will often be pressing and time consuming. Pause for worship will sometimes give the appearance that work is not being done.

The psalmist realized the importance of the regular, systematic, two-way communication with God. He would daily talk with God as well as "eagerly watch" for God. Failure to practice the priority of one's relationship to God may result in your "running dry." In which case you will attempt to do more work to compensate for your neglected relationship to God.

You will be more effective if you will maintain a balance of worship and service. Why not commit yourself now to meet God each morning. You'll be glad you did, and so will He, for it was He who said, "I will make My dwelling among you, and My soul will not reject you. I will also walk among you and be your God, and you shall be My people" (Lev. 26:11-12).

Reader's Response

A Prayer to Complete

Lord, I commit myself to the discipline of meeting You each morning. I know You will be there. Help me to keep my end of this commitment. Especially help me tomorrow morning to . . .

Going Deeper

1. The Bible has many accounts of men and women who met with God for private worship. Beside each Scripture reference list one characteristic of each meeting with God.
   (1) Genesis 5:24 _____
   (2) Genesis 28:15-17 _____
   (3) Isaiah 6:1 _____
   (4) Mark 1:35 _____
   (5) Revelation 1:10 _____
2. Make an application of these scriptural accounts of private worship of these individuals to your service.
   (1) Enoch _____
   (2) Jacob _____
   (3) Isaiah _____
   (4) Jesus _____
   (5) John _____
3. React to the statement: "Your basic priority relationship is to God." Is your worship of God more important than your service to people? Explain your answer.

4. What are three ways you could maintain a "balance" between your worship of God and your service to people?
   (1) _____
   (2) _____
   (3) _____
5. Write a brief covenant (or contract) related to private worship. (Include such items as amount of time spent each day, time of meeting, place of meeting, etc.).

DAY 4 ━━━━━━━━━━━━━━━ DATE _____

Serve Him! Serve Him!

"Serve the Lord with gladness" (Ps. 100:2).

You may not always serve with gladness, but you will always serve. Service will be the content of your days. Remember that you are just as dependent on the power of God for effectiveness in service as you are dependent on Him for anything else in life.

The broad base of Christian service is seen in 1 Peter 4:10-11 which indicates that anything that is a gift from God can be used in service. The discussion of spiritual gifts in 1 Corinthians 12 supports this view.

One of the reasons God calls persons is for service. The nation of Israel was called to serve the nations. John the Baptist was called to serve as a forerunner to Jesus. The disciples were called to serve God in their support of Jesus as well as in sharing the gospel.

Perhaps the best known passage on service is Romans 12:1. It is of interest that *service* is variously translated "reasonable service" (KJV), "spiritual service of worship" (NASB), and "spiritual worship" (NIV). Service and worship are inseparable. A proper balance between worship and service will assist you in serving with gladness.

You will live out your days in the biblical pattern of service, and this service will affect all that you do. Serving with gladness may not always be possible, but it must always be potential.

" 'Take courage,' declares the Lord, 'and work; for I am with you,' says the Lord of hosts" (Hag. 2:4).

Reader's Response

A Prayer to Complete

Father, You showed me how to serve so many times in Your ministry. Help me to find ways to serve You with gladness. I'd like to begin today by serving You through . . .

Going Deeper

1. According to 1 Peter 4:10-11 what is the purpose of using your spiritual gift in the service of God?
2. In 1 Corinthians 12 Paul discussed spiritual gifts. List below two spiritual gifts that God has given you to use in His service. (They do not have to be listed in 1 Corinthians 12.)
   (1) _____
   (2) _____
3. What is your reaction to the various translations to the word *service* in Romans 12:1?
4. List three more ways you could balance your worship of God with your service to persons. (Do not use any of the three listed yesterday.)
   (1) _____
   (2) _____
   (3) _____
5. What are four ways you could assist fellow Christians in serving the Lord with "gladness"?
   (1) _____
   (2) _____
   (3) _____
   (4) _____

DAY 5 ──────────────── DATE ────────────

Quiet Time or Wasted Time

"Cease striving and know that I am God" (Ps. 46:10).

Quiet times are never wasted times. The psalmist indicated we are to "Cease striving" ("Be still," KJV) and acknowledge God. Isaiah said, "In quietness and trust is your strength" (Isa. 30:15), and Jesus asked His disciples to come with Him "to a lonely place and rest a while" (Mark 6:31). Contrary to the pace of our society, Christians must find times to be alone with God.

John Ruskin said that there is no music in a rest, but "the making of music in it." A rest in music is related to the notes that precede it and follow it. So it is in life, the quiet rest is not isolated but integrated into life.

It was during a time of lonely, solitary shepherding of sheep that God first spoke to Moses. In the stillness of a night at Bethel, Jacob had his first personal experience with God. Elijah was associated with winds, earthquakes, and fire, but God spoke to him in a still, small voice. It was in the desert of Arabia that God led Paul after his conversion. And before a momentous day in the life of Jesus, He went to a mountainside for a night of prayer.

There is a difference in rest and idleness. My sixth grade teacher used to say, "An idle mind is the devil's workshop," but God is to be found in rest and solitude. Thus, in the quiet place there is purification and transformation, struggle and encounter. The quiet time with God is not apart from life but rather a part of life.

Reader's Response

A Prayer to Complete

Lord, help me find the time to get away and pray. Today, I especially need a quiet time to . . .

Going Deeper

1. How do you react to the statement: "Quiet times are never wasted times"?
2. In light of the value of the quiet time, suggest two times during your day that you could "be alone with God."
   (1) _____
   (2) _____
3. Seeing how God spoke to Moses, Jacob, Elijah, Paul, and Jesus in quiet, lonely places recall where God first communicated with you, or you were first aware of His communication.
4. Where does God most frequently communicate with you now?
5. The statement "in the quiet place there is purification and transformation, struggle and encounter" needs personalizing. Give an example of each in your own quiet times.
   (1) Purification _____
   (2) Transformation _____
   (3) Struggle _____
   (4) Encounter _____

DAY 6 ━━━━━━━━━━━━━━━ DATE _____
God-Size Vision

"Let us go somewhere else" (Mark 1:38).

Numerous events in the life of Jesus can best be understood by understanding that He was a man of vision. He saw beyond the event into the plan and will of God. One such event that needs this understanding is found in Mark 1:32-38. One day the disciples of Jesus came to a place where they wished to stay. Their Lord had healed many and had cast out demons there in Capernaum. And now the disciples, having interrupted Jesus' early morning private worship time, expressed to Him, "Everyone is looking for you" (v. 37).

What could be better? Here were the people with needs being ministered to by the Master. They loved Him. They sought Him out. They listened to Him. Surely the Kingdom was about to be established right there in Capernaum. Have you ever had a "Capernaum" where all was well? Notice how Jesus responded.

Ignoring the tempting voice that urged Him to stay in Capernaum, Jesus responded with: "Let us go somewhere else to the towns nearby, in order that I may preach there also; for that is what I came out for" (v. 38).

The choice confronts us all. It confronted the children of Israel in Egypt—to move out or stay put. The choice confronted the disciples on the mount of transfiguration—to either erect tents or go back to the people.

Do you stay where you are or go on? Vision kept Jesus from staying where He was. Vision enabled Jesus to see beyond the security of the immediate success—on to other towns and to a cross and an open tomb—and on to a world in need. We are not yet what we are intended to be.

Reader's Response

A Prayer to Complete

O, God of vision, implant within me a vision of Your world and Your will. Enable me to see beyond the present. But, Lord, keep my feet planted in the present, especially . . .

Going Deeper
1. Read Luke's version of this experience in the life of Jesus in Luke 4:42-44. According to Luke, where did Jesus go?
2. Both Mark and Luke describe the place of Jesus' devotion as a "lonely place." Why do you think it was so described?
3. Do you have a "lonely place" where you can be with God to refresh and focus vision? List below three possible places where you could be alone.

(1) _____
(2) _____
(3) _____

4. Name three things that represent the "security of the immediate success" for you.

(1) _____
(2) _____
(3) _____

5. How has your vision led you from the three things listed above to a desire to serve?

6. The reading concludes, "We are not yet what we are intended to be." What are you intended to be?

DAY 7 ━━━━━━━━━━━━ DATE _____

God-Size Vision

"Let us go somewhere else to the towns nearby, in order that I may preach there also; for that is what I came out for" (Mark 1:38).

Just as vision kept Jesus from staying in one place, likewise vision made Him a man of progress. Satan's strategy sometimes causes you to reason: "I'm doing so good where I am, why run the risk? Why not just keep doing what I'm doing?" Often we get our direction confused and hear that reasoning as though it was from God. Just when the disciples were listening to and applying Satan's logic, Jesus began to talk of progress. "Let's go somewhere else to the towns nearby."

Jesus was not just interested in going to "towns nearby." That is progress. Vision made Him a man of progress, but vision also made Him a man with a purpose. He was more interested in the purpose: "that I may preach there also; for that is what I came out for."

One of the most traumatic experiences of childhood was watching a lovable grandmother grab a chicken by the neck and pop its head from its body. Remembering the headless chicken flopping around on the ground brings the thought that the chicken was making progress, but it had no purpose. Vision enabled Jesus not to just progress but to progress with a purpose.

Why do you want to move out? What causes you to desire to minister to others who are now beyond your touch? Check your purpose. For Jesus, the purpose of the progress was wrapped up in His vision of the world and the will of the Father.

Reader's Response

A Prayer to Complete

God, give me a vision today—a vision of Your will for my life—a vision of Your world. Teach me again and again that "where there is no vision, the people perish." Give me an opportunity today to apply my vision especially as it relates to
. . .

Going Deeper

1. Jesus stated, "Let us go somewhere else." How do you see this as progress?
2. How does going to another place of service help the progress of the gospel of Jesus Christ?
3. Compare the purpose of Jesus as recorded by Mark to the purpose as recorded by Luke.
   (1) Mark 1:38 _____
   (2) Luke 4:43 _____
4. Compare the purpose of Jesus (paraphrased in your own words) to your purpose for service.
   (1) Jesus _____
   _____
   (2) Self _____
   _____

5. In one sentence state why you are a Christian servant. This is a statement of your purpose.

DAY 8 ———————————————— DATE ———————

Warning: Mountains Being Moved

"If you have faith as a mustard seed, you shall say to this mountain, 'Move from here to there,' and it shall move" (Matt. 17:20).

The more people meet, the more obvious that faith is the greatest untaped resource Christians have. In fact, many, if not most, of our failures lie here. The disciples were not able to cast out a demon and they asked Jesus, "Why?" He took this occasion to show them the power of faith. An active faith can move mountains, not of itself but as it latches onto the power of God.

Consider the magnitude of some mountains. Jesus referred to "this mountain," no doubt pointing to a nearby mountain. We have all had mountains in our lives, haven't we? Obstacles that humanly speaking could not be moved. But then the mountain mover was employed. Jesus was in the mountain-moving business long before you discovered mountains in your life. He moved social mountains in healing a leper. He moved racial mountains in His encounter with a Syrophoenician woman. He moved sexual mountains in talking with the woman at the well in Sychar. He moved personality mountains in His relationship with men like Peter. He moved religious mountains in His dealings with the Pharisees and Sadduccees.

And He said moving mountains takes only "mustard seed" faith. The mustard seed was the smallest seed the disciples knew about and yet produced the largest herb—sometimes growing to heights of twenty-five feet near the Sea of Galilee. We are often overwhelmed by the bigness of our mountains. Jesus would call our attention to the smallness of the "mustard seed." What is your "mountain" today? On the authority of

God's Word be assured that with just a little bit of faith in Him you can move mountains.
Reader's Response

A Prayer to Complete
Lord, I want to be able to use my faith to move mountains in my own life and in the lives of others. But remind me, Lord, that it is Your power that does the moving, so you determine when and how far. Give me "mustard seed" faith today as I encounter . . .

Going Deeper
1. Note one recent, personal experience where the employment of a little more faith on your part would have changed the results. What do you think the new results would have been?
2. List two "mountains" that exist or have existed in your life. What do you think would happen if you used faith and trusted God to "move" these "mountains"?
   (1) _____
   (2) _____
3. At this point in your life how would you diagnose your faith?
   _____ Critically ill
   _____ Seriously ill
   _____ Stable
   _____ Fair
   _____ Improving
   _____ Well
   _____ Healthy
   _____ Perfect
4. What is one action you could do in the next week to improve the condition of your faith?
5. In Mark's account of this same experience he quotes Jesus

saying, "This kind cannot come out by anything but prayer" (Mark 9:29). What role does prayer play in mountain-moving faith?

DAY 9 ——————————— DATE ——————

Prayer: Why?

"Seek the Lord and His strength;/Seek His face continually" (1 Chron. 16:11).

Why should I pray? I mean, really, doesn't God already know what I'll ask, and doesn't He already know the answer? The first reason for prayer is that the Old Testament teaches it. Adam and Eve prayed. Abraham was a man of prayer. Jacob prayed when he encountered the angel. Moses was the prince of intercessory prayer. The Israelites prayed in Egypt. Solomon prayed concerning the Temple. The psalmist prayed and sang of prayer. Job prayed. Each of the prophets communicated with God through prayer. If prayer was ever important for the chosen people of God, it still is.

A second reason for prayer is that the New Testament teaches it. Jesus prayed at His baptism. He prayed for His disciples as well as for others such as Lazarus. He prayed before feeding the 5,000 and at other miracles. He prayed more and more toward the end of His earthly ministry, on the mount of transfiguration, in the garden, at the Last Supper, and finally He prayed while dying on the cross. Paul and his associates lived and ministered in continual communication through prayer.

Finally, our lives require a relationship to God through prayer. Prayer has been defined as experiencing the presence of God. It is a love relationship. The purpose is not to get answers, for God knows what you need before you ask. The purpose is to draw closer to God. Prayer is not seeking the gifts of God but rather seeking God. Prayer is an absolute necessity for the people of God.

Reader's Response

A Prayer to Complete

Lord, teach me that it is not nearly as important that I know why I pray as it is that I do pray. May I learn more about You today as I pray. Now my prayer is . . .

Going Deeper

1. Other than the examples given, can you list two other biblical characters who were recognized for their prayer life?

    (1) _____

    (2) _____

2. The writer said, "The purpose is not to get answers, for God knows what you need before you ask. The purpose is to draw closer to God." How do you react to this?

3. Write your own definition of prayer.

4. On the scale below rate your present prayer life consistency with an X and where you'd like to be with an O. What will you need to do to move from X to O?

    Nonexistent   Consistent

    |——|——|——|——|——|——|——|——|——|

5. List five reasons why you ought to have a consistent prayer life.

    (1) _____

    (2) _____

    (3) _____

    (4) _____

    (5) _____

DAY 10 ──────────────── DATE _____
Prayer: To Whom

"Pray to God" (Job 33:26).

We understand that we are to pray, but to whom should we address our prayer? Several places in the New Testament we are told to pray to the Father, "for through Him we both have our access in one Spirit to the Father" (Eph. 2:18). Matthew 6:6 says, "When you pray, go into your inner room, and when you have shut your door, pray to your Father who is in secret, and your Father who sees in secret will repay you." In what we call the "Lord's Prayer," our Lord began with "Our Father" (Luke 11:2, KJV).

The New Testament also says that we are to pray to the Son, Jesus Christ. Romans 10:12 says that the "Lord" is "abounding in riches for all who call upon Him." Paul prayed to the Lord three times concerning his thorn in the flesh (2 Cor. 12:8). Jesus said, "Whatever you ask in My name, that will I do" (John 14:13).

But the New Testament also makes references to praying with the help of the Holy Spirit; in fact, "We do not know how to pray as we should, but the Spirit Himself intercedes for us" (Rom. 8:26). On another occasion, Paul wrote, "With all prayer and petition pray at all times in the Spirit" (Eph. 6:18).

So to whom should we address our prayers? The answer is: All of the above. Be assured of one thing—there is no jealously within the Godhead. When you pray, the Father, the Son, and the Holy Spirit hear you.

Reader's Response

A Prayer to Complete

God, may I not get hung up on to whom I address my prayer but be faithful in my prayer life. Teach me that Father, Son, and Spirit are all listening and willing to communicate with me. Today I would like to communicate the following . . .

28

Going Deeper

1. In your past experiences, with whom have you addressed your prayers? Why?
2. React to the feeling that "there is no jealousy within the Godhead. When you pray, the Father, the Son, and the Holy Spirit hear you."
3. Voice two prayer requests to the Trinity.

   (1) _____

   (2) _____

DAY 11 ━━━━━━━━━━━━━━━ DATE _____

Prayer: When?

"And when you are praying" (Matt. 6:7).

Did you ever have a day when you just couldn't find time to pray? Or you got to the end of the day and realized that you had not prayed all day? We're usually so involved that we have to break our pattern in order to pray. In the New Testament, it was different. God was frequently having to stop a prayer meeting to get His people to act. When the Holy Spirit came on the Day of Pentecost, the first thing He had to do was interrupt a prayer meeting. So, when should we pray?

The Bible teaches that we should have regular set times for prayer. Daniel prayed three times a day (Dan. 6:10). Likewise the psalmist prayed at evening, morning, and at noon (Ps. 55:17). On another occasion the psalmist said he prayed "by day and in the night" (Ps. 88:1). In Mark 1:35, we are told that Jesus prayed early in the morning. Acts 3:1 indicates that "Peter and John were going up to the temple at the ninth hour, the hour of prayer." Pray at regular set times.

The Bible also teaches that we are to pray continually. Luke 21:36 says, "Keep on the alert at all times, praying in order that you may have strength." First Thessalonians 5:17 says to "pray without ceasing." Jesus told a parable to His followers "to show that at all times they ought to pray" (Luke 18:1). Prior to Pentecost the disciples "were continually devoting themselves to prayer" (Acts 1:14). Paul admonished the Ephesians to "pray at all times" (6:18). Finally, in Luke 6:12 we are told that on one occasion Jesus "spent the whole night in prayer."

How many friends do you have whom you can call on at any hour of the day or night and call on continually? God is always listening. Take advantage of it.

Reader's Response

A Prayer to Complete

God, forgive me for missing so many opportunities to communicate with You. May You and I today be in regular and continual communication. Let's begin with . . .

Going Deeper

1. When was the last day you spent without having time to pray during the day? List the reasons why you were unable to pray.
   (1) _____
   (2) _____
   (3) _____
2. Could any of the above reasons have been dissolved by a regular set time for prayer each day?
3. List the advantages of setting and keeping a regular time of prayer.
   (1) _____
   (2) _____
   (3) _____
   (4) _____
4. List the advantages of spontaneous prayer at various times during the day.
   (1) _____
   (2) _____

(3) _____

(4) _____

5. Is there any advantage to a daily balance between set times for prayer and spontaneous prayer? If so, what is the advantage?

DAY 12 ──────────────── DATE _____

Prayer: For What?

"Father, . . . glorify Thy Son. . . . Keep them in Thy name. . . . I do not ask in behalf of these alone, but for those also who believe in Me through their word" (John 17:1,11,20).

For what shall you pray? Is it all right to pray for what you really want? A study of the prayers in the Book of Acts provides an interesting fact. Not one time in Acts is anyone reported to have prayed for oneself but always for others or for the cause of Christ. A study of the prayers of the New Testament writers provides further information. Read Colossians 1:9-12; Romans 1:9-10; Ephesians 1:15-19; Philippians 1:3-11; 1 Thessalonians 1:2; 1 Timothy 2:1-2; Philemon 4-6; Hebrews 13:18-19; and 3 John 1:2. You will notice that these writers prayed for other believers, not for themselves or for nonbelievers. Paul offered one personal prayer, and that was offered in the midst of ministry (2 Cor. 12:8-9).

What about the model prayers offered by Jesus? In the Lord's Prayer, He taught His disciples to pray for the Kingdom and for themselves (Matt. 6:9-13; Luke 11:2-4). In the High Priestly Prayer, Jesus prayed for Himself, for His disciples, and for all who in the future would believe on Him (John 17:1-26). And in Gethsemane Jesus prayed for Himself and for the Kingdom (Matt. 26:36-48).

No New Testament prayer seems to be complete without intercession on behalf of others. This seems to be the top priority. We have prayed for everything conceivable, however, and God has listened. He is not a "picky" God, but He desires that we be concerned and pray for others and for the Kingdom —the people of God—and not just for personal requests.

Reader's Response

A Prayer to Complete

God, I have asked for many things in my past prayers. Today, I pray for the world around me, especially for those who are a part of Your forever family. Help me today to pray honestly for . . .

Going Deeper

1. What was the object of prayer in each of the following instances?
   (1) Colossians 1:9-12_____
   (2) Romans 1:9-10_____
   (3) Ephesians 1:15-19 _____
   (4) Philippians 1:3-11 _____
   (5) 1 Thessalonians 1:2_____
   (6) 1 Timothy 2:1-2 _____
   (7) Philemon 4-6 _____
   (8) Hebrews 13:18-19 _____
   (9) 3 John 1:2_____
2. Why do you think it is never recorded that the New Testament writers prayed for themselves?
3. What was the occasion for Paul's personal prayer in 2 Corinthians 12? Is there any application to be made to your prayer life from this?
4. The writer stated, "We have prayed for everything conceivable, however, and God has listened." List some of the things you have prayed for recently that were not top priority items. How did God deal with these items?
   (1) _____
   (2) _____

(3) _____

(4) _____

(5) _____

DAY 13 ─────────────── DATE _____
Prayer: Where?"

"In every place . . . pray" (1 Tim. 2:8).

When you pray in public, do you ever wish people weren't listening? Well, when should you really pray? The Bible teaches that we are to sometimes pray in public. The disciples prayed in public worship services (Acts 4:31). They learned this from Jesus who also believed in public prayer and prayed at the feeding of the multitude (Mark 8:6) and at the raising of Lazarus (John 11:38-45). Paul likewise believed in public prayer. In Acts 27:35, Paul "took bread and gave thanks to God in the presence of all."

But the Bible also teaches that we are to pray in private. Jesus said, "When you pray, you are not be as the hypocrites; for they love to stand and pray in the synagogues and on the street corners, in order to be seen by men. Truly I say to you, they have their reward in full. But you, when you pray, go into your inner room, and when you have shut your door, pray to your Father" (Matt. 6:5-6). Prior to the Lord's Prayer, Jesus was praying in "a certain place" (Luke 11:1). This seemed to be the pattern of Jesus. Luke tells us "He Himself would often slip away to the wilderness and pray" (Luke 5:16).

So, where do you pray? The answer is both of the above. First Timothy 2:8 says, "Therefore I want the men in every place to pray."

33

Reader's Response

A Prayer to Complete

God, do You really care that much where I am when I pray? Or are You more concerned that I really pray? Help me today "in every place to pray." Now in this place I pray that
. . .

Going Deeper

1. In the following public prayers, what was the main thrust of each prayer?
   (1) Acts 4:23-31 _____
   (2) Mark 8:6 _____
   (3) John 11:41-42 _____
   (4) Acts 27:35 _____
2. What personal application could you draw from the above as to your own public prayers?
3. What was the result of each public prayer?
   (1) Acts 4:31-35 _____
   (2) Mark 8:6-9 _____
   (3) John 11:43-44 _____
   (4) Acts 27:35-36 _____
4. From the above answers, what could you expect as a result of your public prayers?
5. From the references to Jesus praying in private (Matt. 6:5-6; Luke 11:1; Luke 5:16), what can you apply to your private prayer life?

34

DAY 14 ———————————— DATE _____
Prayer: Expecting What?

"And everything you ask in prayer, believing, you shall receive" (Matt. 21:22).

Do you pray, expecting an answer? You should! Every prayer to God is answered. Sometimes God's answer is no. Prior to His death, Jesus prayed in the garden of Gethsemane, "Let this cup pass from Me." His was an honest request to postpone the cross. The Father's answer was no (Matt. 26:36-48; Mark 14:32-42; Luke 22:39-46). You will make many honest requests (2 Cor. 12:8-9). Occasionally, the answer will be no, but the prayer will have been answered. Expect an answer when you pray.

Sometimes God's answer to prayer is: "wait" or "not yet." It is this conditional answer that is most difficult to cope with. After the crucifixion and resurrection of Jesus, the disciples were no doubt ready for service—ready to conquer the world. Although not recorded, surely the disciples asked about the future. Jesus responded to this unrecorded request, "Tarry ye in the city of Jerusalem, until ye be endued with power from on high" (Luke 24:49, KJV). Occasionally, we make a prayer request for service, and the response is "tarry" or "wait," but the prayer is answered. Expect an answer when you pray.

Sometimes God's answer to prayer is yes. Jesus said to ask, and we would receive (Matt. 7:7-11). In Acts 4:31, "When they had prayed, the place where they had gathered together was shaken, and they were all filled with the Holy Spirit." James 5:17 tells us that Elijah prayed that it would not rain for three and a half years, and he prayed again, and it rained. On some occasions we will pray and God will answer with a yes. God always answers prayer. Expect an answer when you pray.

Reader's Response

A Prayer to Complete
God, help me to pray expectantly. Teach me that You are ever present both to hear and to answer my prayers today. Today I pray . . .

Going Deeper
1. Give a recent experience in your prayer life when God's answer to your request was . . .
   (1) No _____
   (2) Wait _____
   (3) Yes _____
2. State your reaction to the statement: "Every prayer to God is answered."
3. The experience of Jesus in Matthew 21:18-22 brings forth His statement, "And everything you ask in prayer, believing, you shall receive." Does the context of the experience surrounding this quote help you understand its meaning? What did Jesus mean?
4. Make a prayer list. In the right-hand column place the date of the answer to your request. In the middle column place an *N* for a no answer, a *W* for a wait answer, or a *Y* for a yes answer. Refer to this page as time progresses, and God deals with these requests.

Request	Answer	Date Answered
(1)		
(2)		
(3)		
(4)		
(5)		

DAY 15 ———————————————— DATE _____
Prayer: How?

"Keep watching and praying" (Mark 14:38).

Have you ever wondered how you should pray? Here are a few suggestions. Three times (Mark 14:36; Rom. 8:15; Gal. 4:6) in the New Testament God is addressed as "Abba! Father!" *Abba* is a personal, intimate word. An English equivalent would be *Daddy*. *Father* is a word of respect and dignity. Address God both personally and with respect.

There is not a set posture for prayer in the Bible. In Matthew 4:9 Jesus was told by Satan to "fall down and worship me." The kneeling position is mentioned in Acts 20:36; Acts 7:60; Acts 9:40; and Ephesians 3:14-16. In Matthew 6:5, standing is mentioned as a prayer posture.

Somewhere in your prayer life you should include the basic forms of prayer: adoration, confession, thanksgiving, supplication, petition, intercession, and commitment.

There is no set wording or pattern of the wording of prayers in the Bible although they seem to be conversational. Prayer is communication, two-way communication. How long has it been since you "listened" a prayer rather than "voicing" a prayer?

Perhaps the best suggestion is to pray as Jesus did, "not what I will, but what Thou wilt" (Mark 14:36). When all else is said and done concerning prayer, it is God who answers in His own time and in His own will. So, therefore, keep praying! And leave the particulars up to God.
Reader's Response

A Prayer to Complete

God, teach me to pray. But help me to go on praying as I learn. May Your will be done on earth today in my life and circumstances even as it is done in heaven. I particularly would like to see your will done in regard to . . .

Going Deeper
1. How do you address God when you pray? Is it a term of intimacy? Of respect? What might be a better (or another) term you could use to address God?
2. What position do you use in prayer? Try kneeling the next time you pray and record any significant results or feelings?
3. If you were to write your next prayer, what would you include in the following areas?
   (1) Adoration _____
   (2) Confession _____
   (3) Thanksgiving _____
   (4) Supplication _____
   (5) Petition _____
   (6) Intercession _____
   (7) Commitment _____
4. Write a prayer to God of approximately twenty-five words in length. As you reflect on what you have written, allow "listening" time, so God can communicate with you. Record any results or feelings.

_____

_____

_____

DAY 16 ——————————— DATE _____
God's Will
"The mind of man plans his way,/But the Lord directs his steps" (Prov. 16:9).

In more than twenty years of ministry, one issue has remained in the forefront. Times have changed, people have changed, locations have changed, I have changed, but the question is still the same. Whatever the age, whatever the situation in life, the question is basically the same, "How can

I know the will of God?" The specifics—job, career, spouse, family—vary, but the question remains.

Obviously, there are no easy answers, and certainly none that could be dealt with on one page. The problem apparently is as old as the Old Testament, but the answer is as fresh as the first time you read Proverbs 16:9. Basically, one must ask God for leadership, then plan for the future. You go with what you know to be God's will, and you trust your decisions are God led in the "grey areas" of uncertainty.

To discover and follow God's will is the greatest comfort known to man. In God's will you have every right to call upon God for help in every circumstance, good or bad. If God led you in, God will lead you through. The person who finds and follows God's will finds supreme security for "the Lord directs his steps."

What if you miss God's will? If you miss it on purpose, you pay the obvious consequences, but what if you sincerely try to follow God's will and miss it? Then you discover the God of the second chance. God never punishes sincerity, nor does He forsake the sincerely wrong. Get over the guilt, and get on with life. Make your plans, but don't set them in concrete. It is God who "directs" your steps.

Reader's Response

A Prayer to Complete

God, help me do what I know is right to do, and guide me in the unknown areas of my life such as . . .

Going Deeper

1. What aspect of God's will—job, career, spouse, family, etc. —is causing the most concern in your life at present?

2. What do you understand to be God's leadership in the above area of concern?

3. What advice do you receive from trusted and respected friends related to the above area of concern?
4. What are your own feelings about the above area of concern? Try to picture in your mind how it would be in each alternative decision available to you.
5. On the basis of answers to the above questions, what is needed before a decision is made in regard to God's will in the area of your concern? What are the "grey areas"?

DAY 17 ——————————— DATE _____
Dealing with Difficulties

"We are afflicted in every way, but not crushed; perplexed, but not despairing; persecuted, but not forsaken; struck down, but not destroyed" (2 Cor. 4:8-9).

Reading between the lines on her face, I found more difficulties than she would verbalize to me. Her setbacks were numerous, her victories, few. I wanted to tell her that the only people without difficulties are those buried in cemeteries, but somehow that didn't appear to be appropriate or helpful. I had known for a long time that every person I met was carrying a cross, but hers seemed to be larger than most. So I made several suggestions.

Learn to resist temptation because it will come. Stop feeling guilty because of temptation. Temptation is not sin but rather, human. To experience no temptation is to fail to be fully human. Yielding to temptation is sin. Like Jesus, who also faced temptation, learn to resist.

Work at difficulties with the vision of succeeding. Two frogs fell into a vat of cream. One gave up and died. The other struggled and churned and turned the cream into butter, then hopped off. To make no provision for your own failure is to allow God to make every provision for your success.

And don't forget the power of prayer. Continue to take your

burden to the cross, leave it there, and stop going back to check on it. God is able to handle your burden without your help. Let Him.

You, like my burdened friend, cannot always choose your difficulties, but you can choose your response to the difficulties.

Reader's Response

A Prayer to Complete

Lord, help me today to choose well my response to the difficulties that seem to get in my way; in particular, help me deal with . . .

Going Deeper

1. Identify a current area of difficulty in your life.

   _____

   _____

2. What are the temptations related to your area of difficulty? What sources of strength do you have available to you in resisting these temptations?

3. What steps could you take that would lead to success related to your area of difficulty?

4. React to the statement: "To make no provision for your own failure is to allow God to make every provision for your success."

5. Write a twenty-five-word prayer related to your area of difficulty:

   _____

   _____

   _____

6. How do you feel about the fact that you "cannot always choose your difficulties, but you can choose your response to the difficulties"?

DAY 18 ———————————— DATE ———————

What Did God Get When God Got . . . Ruth?

"All that you say I will do" (Ruth 3:5).

Ruth, a Moabite girl, was the widowed daughter-in-law of Naomi. She wept when Naomi asked her if she wanted to leave and return to her own people. There was security in staying with Naomi. With enough respect for Naomi to do whatever was asked of her, Ruth got the attention of a rich relative, Boaz. Boaz was impressed and took the necessary steps to make Ruth his wife. As the wife of Boaz, Ruth became the mother of Obed and the great-grandmother of King David, placing her in the direct line of the Messiah.

Several important applications can be made from Ruth's life. In spite of a low self-image that caused her to see herself as "just a foreigner" and that caused her to wonder why anyone would be good to her, Ruth made herself available to God. She had an unquestioning faith in God and in God's people. She allowed more mature believers to advise her.

One is caused to wonder what would have happened if Ruth had gone back to Moab with her sister-in-law Orpah rather than staying with Naomi. Because she did stay and make herself available, God chose to place her in the direct line of His Son, Jesus Christ. So important was she that Matthew listed her in his genealogy of Jesus in Matthew 1:5-6. Ruth teaches us wonderful lessons on love, devotion, and faith, but possibly the greatest lesson to be gained from the life of Ruth is one of availability. Regardless of who you are (or who you are not), if you will make yourself available, God will use you.

Reader's Response

A Prayer to Complete

God, I want to make myself available to You right now. Regardless of my own self-image, take me and use me as You will. I am especially available today in the area of . . .

Going Deeper

1. From Ruth 1—4 make a list of eight characteristics of Ruth.
   (1) _____
   (2) _____
   (3) _____
   (4) _____
   (5) _____
   (6) _____
   (7) _____
   (8) _____

2. Which of the above characteristics could be applied to your life?

3. Of the above characteristics in Ruth's life and in your life, select one and think how God could use that characteristic this week.

4. Ruth allowed more mature believers to advise her. List three more mature believers who could advise you.
   (1) _____
   (2) _____
   (3) _____

5. Ruth's response to Naomi in Ruth 1:16-17 is a beautiful description of trust. Apply the statement to your following of Jesus Christ.

DAY 19 ———————— DATE _____

What Did God Get When God Got . . . Naomi?

"All the city was stirred because of them, and the women said, 'Is this Naomi?' " (Ruth 1:19).

As the wife of Elimelech, Naomi of Bethlehem had borne two sons, Mahlon and Chilion. Their early deaths had left Naomi with two widowed daughters-in-law, Ruth and Orpah. After all three of the women had been widowed, Naomi offered Ruth and Orpah an opportunity to return to their home. Ruth chose to remain with Naomi.

Naomi suffered from a low self-image. She felt that she was not capable of keeping Ruth as well as someone else could. She was emotional, twice weeping (1:9,14). She didn't think she was young enough to find a husband. She said, "Call me Mara" (bitter) and felt that God had turned His back on her (1:21).

But God used Naomi. She never made the headlines, but she quietly encouraged Ruth, first to work in the field of Boaz, then to marry him. Ruth 3:18 indicates that Naomi taught Ruth patience. Naomi was respected by the women of the city who came to her for advice (4:14-15). She teaches all of us a lesson in concern.

Her quiet patience and trust in God paid dividends in the life of Ruth but also in her own life as she became the great, great-grandmother of King David. That which Naomi passed on to Ruth may well be thought of as an early form of discipling. We learn from Naomi that patient faith and trust, plus a lack of desire for the "spotlight" plus a willingness to serve in spite of low self-image, equals blessings from God and spiritual reproduction.

Reader's Response

A Prayer to Complete

Lord, sometimes I identify with Naomi. I wonder, "Why me?" Help me to be aware today of the "Ruths" who are around me. Help me to minister to persons today without desiring the "spotlight." Especially help me minister to . . .

Going Deeper

1. From the Book of Ruth list three ways God used Naomi.

(1) _____

(2) _____

(3) _____

2. Could God use you in any of the above ways? If so, make the proper applications to your situation.

3. Naomi affirmed Ruth on several occasions in Ruth's life. List below two persons whom you could affirm this week. Record the date and results in the right-hand column.

	Person	*Results*
(1)		
(2)		

4. The statement concerning Naomi, "She never made the headlines" is applicable to your situation. Write below one act that you could do for someone that would encourage that person. In order to avoid the "headlines" or the "spotlight," do not tell them that you performed the act. Record your feelings below also.

DAY 20 ━━━━━━━━━━━━━ DATE _____
What Did God Get When God Got . . . Amos?

"I am not. . . . But the Lord took me" (Amos 7:14-15).

Amos was a common man, a sheepherder from Tekoa (1:1), who lived during the days of King Uzziah in Judah and Jeroboam in Israel (approximately 765 BC). Amos was not a prophet, nor the son of a prophet when first called by God (7:14), but was a poor man who in addition to his job herding sheep, held a second job as a keeper of sycamore figs (7:14). In spite of his common, simple background, God called him to be a prophet (7:15).

God used Amos to pronounce judgment upon Damascus, Philistia, Tyre, Edom, Amma, Moab, Judah, and Israel. Amos was used to warn God's people in Israel to "prepare to meet God" (4:12). He envisioned destruction from God through locust, drought, and measurement (7:1-9). He was a champion of social justice and described the end of Israel (8:8-14).

In the midst of this prophecy of doom, Amos offered elements of hope. He encouraged the people to seek God and live (5:6). He prophesied that God would "raise up the fallen booth of David" and rebuild it (9:11), and that great days of prosperity would come for God's people (9:13-15).

Many common men have been called by God to accomplish uncommon tasks. Amos had very little going for him except that God had called him apart for a special purpose. When God calls you, background makes little difference, for God is bigger than your background.

Reader's Response

A Prayer to Complete

God, whatever I have as a background in my life, I give to You right now. Be it small or great, You are capable of using it or working around it—whichever is necessary. Help me today to feel Your "call" stronger than I feel anything else. I will be especially attentive to your call in . . .

Going Deeper

1. From Amos 5:4-15 and 9:7-15, what elements of hope did Amos give the people?

    (1) _____
    (2) _____
    (3) _____
    (4) _____

2. From Amos 7:14-17, what do you learn about Amos?

    (1) _____
    (2) _____
    (3) _____
    (4) _____
    (5) _____

3. God used Amos in spite of his background. What are some

negative elements in your background that God can work through in order to use you?

(1) _____

(2) _____

(3) _____

4. What are some positive elements in your background that God can use?

(1) _____

(2) _____

(3) _____

5. Reflect on the statement: "God is bigger than your background."

DAY 21 ━━━━━━━━━━ DATE _____

What Did God Get When God Got . . . Caleb?

"But My servant Caleb . . . I will bring into the land which he entered, and his descendants shall take possession of it" (Num. 14:24).

Who was Caleb? Numbers 13 informs us that he was the son of Jephunneh and was one of the twelve spies sent by Moses to the Promised Land of Canaan. The Israelites having crossed the Red Sea out of Egyptian slavery and having received the law at Mount Sinai were now ready to conquer the land of Canaan. But of the twelve spies, only Joshua and Caleb returned with a favorable report. It is extremely difficult for God's people to move forward when more than 80 percent of the leadership is opposed. Forty years later, only Joshua and Caleb, of all the Israelite men of fighting age, remained to enter the Promised Land (Num. 14:20-24, 38). The "land of promise" belongs to those who not only profess their faith in God but who are ready and willing to possess the land.

So, why did God want Caleb? Several reasons are evident from the Scriptures. He was a courageous man. In the midst of near riot and rebellion, it was Caleb who "quieted the people" (Num. 13:30;14:6-9). He had a "different spirit" and followed God fully. The difference between the ten spies and the two spies was the "spirit" within them (Num. 14:24). He was realistic but confident. While the majority were expressing the fear of failure, Caleb said, "We shall surely overcome it" (Num. 13:30). He lived on when the other spies perished. Those who brought the negative report died in a plague (Num. 14:37-38). Caleb followed God fully (Deut. 1:36; Josh. 14:6-14). He conquered that which was assigned to him (Josh. 15:14). Finally, he saved his family (Deut. 1:36).

Two questions of personal application: First, has God got you? Does He really have all of you? Second, what has God got now that He's got you?

Reader's Response

A Prayer to Complete

Father, thank You for leaders like Caleb whose faith stand the test of the opposition. I need to learn more about that kind of faith. Grant me the courage to stand firm for and move forward on that which I believe is from you. May I apply my faith today as I . . .

Going Deeper

1. God's intent was for His people to possess the land. From Numbers 13:30 to 14:25 list some reasons why God could use Caleb in this endeavor.

   (1) _____
   (2) _____
   (3) _____
   (4) _____

2. For you, what would be the application of "possess the land"? In other words, what is God's goal or plan for you?

3. The writer states, "The 'land of promise' belongs to those

who not only profess their faith in God but who are ready and willing to possess the land." List three ways you are "professing your faith."

(1) _____

(2) _____

(3) _____

4. Now list three ways that you are "possessing the land."

(1) _____

(2) _____

(3) _____

5. What could you do today or tomorrow that would allow God to accomplish His purpose for you?

DAY 22 ———————————————— DATE _____

What Did God Get When God Got . . . Titus?

"To Titus, my true child in a common faith" (Titus 1:4).

Titus was a young man with potential. Paul was so concerned about Titus while in Troas that he went to Macedonia looking for him (2 Cor. 2:13). Titus was loved by the Corinthian Christians (2 Cor. 7:13-16). He was eager to help (2 Cor. 8:16) and went with Paul and Barnabas to Jerusalem on one occasion (Gal. 2:1). Paul thought so highly of him as to leave him in Crete in charge of the work there (Titus 1:5) and wrote the New Testament Letter to Titus which carries his name. Titus, probably because of Paul's urging, went to Dalmatia just before Paul's death (2 Tim. 4:10). He was a partner and helper with Paul (2 Cor. 8:23) and is called by Paul his true son in the faith (Titus 1:4).

God used Titus to encourage Paul in Macedonia with good news from Corinth (2 Cor. 7:5-7) and to comfort Paul towards the end of his life (Titus 3:12).

It is rather obvious that Paul saw a great deal of potential in Titus, but he saw more than potential. Some young people have all the potential in the world. They've got it all going for them. They are limited only by themselves. Titus was such a person. But more than this, Titus was teachable. The life of Paul indicates that he would not have spent this much time with one who was not teachable.

Potential plus self-assurance or conceit or self-pride equals less than the best and possibly even failure in God's eyes if uncorrected. Potential plus teachability equals a person that God can use.

Reader's Response

A Prayer to Complete

Father, I'm not sure how much potential You think I have, but I do want to be teachable. Teach Lord; Your servant is listening. I need to be teachable today in the area of . . .

Going Deeper

1. In 2 Corinthians 7:5-7 we are told that Titus encouraged Paul. Below, name one person, and describe how you could encourage that person in the next three days. Record your feelings and the results after you have encouraged them.
   Person to be encouraged _____

Process	*Results/Feelings*

2. The writer described some persons as "limited only by themselves." What are three ways you limit yourself?
   (1) _____
   (2) _____
   (3) _____

3. Titus allowed God to use him by refusing to limit himself. How could you remove the three limitations on yourself which you've listed above?

(1) _____
(2) _____
(3) _____

4. Perhaps the greatest quality of Titus was that he was teachable. List below two lessons that you have been taught recently and the person who taught you the lesson.

             Lesson   *Teacher*

(1) _____   _____
(2) _____   _____

5. "Potential plus teachability equals a person that God can use." What is one thing you could do today or tomorrow that would give God a better chance in using you?

DAY 23 ————————————— DATE _____
Prayerorities

"If my people, which are called by my name, shall . . . pray" (2 Chron. 7:14, KJV).

What do you call those things which you pray for most frequently and most earnestly? You know—your "top ten" prayer list—those requests which seem to take priority over all other requests. Let's coin a new word, shall we? Those top priority prayers we will call "prayerorities." Now what are your "prayerorities"? A few suggestions might get you started.

Pray that God's kingdom will come and His will be done not only on earth but in your life even as it is done in heaven.

Pray that those whom you touch today and those who touch you will know of God's presence in their lives and may experience His redeeming power.

Pray that Jesus Christ will be lifted up in everything you do today, in everything you say today, indeed, even in everything you think today.

Pray that your vision will be increased and focused on a

world around you in need of a Savior and that you will see yourself as a servant-messenger of God's saving grace.

Pray for a consistency of life-style evangelism and ministry in your own life that results in a continual rebirth of persons into the family of God.

Reader's Response

A Prayer to Complete

Lord, thank you for the high privilege of prayer. In addition to these printed "prayerorities," I come before you today with these of my own beginning with . . .

Going Deeper

1. What would need to happen for God's kingdom to come and His will to be done in your life today?
2. List three persons who have experienced God's presence in the last week because of you.
   (1) _____
   (2) _____
   (3) _____
3. What are two ways you could "lift" Jesus up in the next three days?
   (1) _____
   (2) _____
4. What would need to happen before your vision could be increased?
5. Who was the last person to become a Christian as a result of your witness and ministry? _____
   How long ago was it?_____
6. What would you have to do to increase your life-style of evangelism and ministry?

DAY 24 ——————————————— DATE _____

Success in Spite of Circumstances

"The God of heaven will give us success" (Neh. 2:20).

Nehemiah asked about the conditions of the Jews who were in Jerusalem. He was told, "The remnant there in the province who survived the captivity are in great distress" (Neh. 1:3). One thing Nehemiah knew he would face even before he went to Jerusalem was a distressed people. Everywhere you go to serve God, you will find that some of God's people are in distress. You need to give to them a word of hope.

After arriving in Jerusalem, Nehemiah made a night ride around the city only to discover a second major problem. "So I went out at night by the Valley Gate . . . inspecting the walls of Jerusalem which were broken down" (Neh. 2:13). In that day of walled cities, this was their chief defense against the enemy. No longer was Jerusalem safe from attack. Its defenses were broken down, and as a result they were easy prey for their enemies. You need to help rebuild some walls, for people under Satan's attack.

Finally, as Nehemiah led the people to begin rebuilding the walls of Jerusalem, he encountered a third problem. "They mocked us and despised us" (Neh. 2:19). There will be in most attempts for God a group of persons, some of whom mean well, who will mock and despise God's servants. Get ready for them.

In spite of the circumstances encountered along the way you, as a servant of God, have an answer for the critics. It is the same answer that Nehemiah had. Tell them, as well as the distressed Christians and those whose walls have fallen, "The God of heaven will give us success; therefore we His servants will arise and build" (Neh. 2:20).

Reader's Response

A Prayer to Complete

Father, may I be able to pass on a good word to the distressed and the defenseless and the dissenters. And may I be able to

pass it on from personal experience. So let me experience success in my own life today as I pass on encouragement to
. . .

Going Deeper

1. From Nehemiah 1:1-3 and 2:1-5 why were the people in distress?
   - (1) _____
   - (2) _____
   - (3) _____
   - (4) _____

2. What are three reasons why people are in distress today especially the people with whom you work?
   - (1) _____
   - (2) _____
   - (3) _____

3. In Nehemiah's day the walls of Jerusalem were broken down. What are some things that are broken down in our day, and how can you help to rebuild?
   - (1) _____
   - (2) _____
   - (3) _____

4. From Nehemiah 2:17-20, why do you think the believers were "mocked" and "despised"?

5. What are some reasons believers today are "mocked" and "despised"?

6. Name one person that you could speak to in the next three days who is either distressed, defenseless, or dissenting. _____ Commit yourself to speaking a word of encouragement to that person.

54

Qualifications for Followship (1)

"If anyone wishes to come after Me, let him deny himself" (Luke 9:23).

The testing in Caesarea Phillippi marked a turning point in Jesus' relation to His disciples. From that time on, Jesus began to reveal more and more of His purpose to the disciples. From that point in His ministry, they went on to the mount of transfiguration, but before going on Jesus set forth three basic qualifications for those who would follow Him.

Qualification number one set forth by Jesus for the one who would follow Him was to "let him deny himself" (Luke 9:23). We know little about self-denial, but this is more than giving up a meal or a habit for a period of time. "To deny" means to treat as though nonexistent. This is where our Christian experience begins. We became a Christian when we denied ourselves the right to be Lord of our own lives. Self-denial means I give up self and treat self as though nonexistent in order to exist for Jesus Christ.

Not only does our Christian experience begin here, but our spiritual growth continues here. To grow physically, I must deny myself some things—too much food, too little sleep, etc. To grow spiritually, I must enter into a process of self-denial. I cannot grow of myself. God alone causes growth in a believer. Life must be more and more of Jesus and less and less of self.

"He must increase, but I must decrease" (John 3:30). Thus Jesus set forth the first qualification for followship. Tarry here until this one is settled. To go further without settling this qualification is a vain effort.

Reader's Response

A Prayer to Complete

Lord, I want to deny myself. I really do. But it is so hard. You knew it would be difficult, didn't You? You planned it that way, didn't You? Did You want me to be sure before I said yes to following You? Help me, Lord, today to deny myself especially in relation to . . .

Going Deeper
1. Contrast and compare your reaction to the statement of Jesus "If anyone wishes to come after Me, let him deny himself" with how you think the disciples might have felt when they first heard it.
2. What are two areas of your life where you need to "deny yourself"?
    (1) _____
    (2) _____
3. React to the statement: "God alone causes growth in a believer."
4. What could you do that would allow God the freedom to cause growth in your life?
5. How can you "decrease" and Jesus "increase" without destroying your own self-worth?

DAY 26 ——————— DATE _____
Qualifications for Followship (2)
"If anyone wishes to come after Me, let him . . . take up his cross daily" (Luke 9:23).

Not only must one "deny himself" if one wishes to follow Jesus, he or she must also heed the second qualification for followship, which is to "take up his cross daily" (Luke 9:23).

Tradition in Jesus' day called for the condemned to carry his own cross to the place of crucifixion. This was done amidst a great deal of shame and mockery. Often, the condemned was abused physically not to mention the mental and emotional torment involved. We have too often glorified the cross of Jesus to the point that we have sometimes forgotten that He "for the joy set before Him endured the cross, despising the shame" (Heb. 12:2). The cross in the New Testament was not what we have sometimes made it to be. The cross was an object of death.

There are two crosses in the New Testament. There is the cross that Jesus shouldered and on which He died. But there is also the cross to which Jesus referred when He said if a person wished to follow Him, that person should "take up his cross." Our cross, too, is an object of death. To take up your cross means to die to yourself.

Of special significance is the word *daily* in Luke's account of Jesus' statement. The cross involves daily discipline. Perhaps that's what Paul meant when he said, "I die daily" (1 Cor. 15:31). The real measure of followship is not in the great moments but in the daily cross bearing of the follower. How are you doing with your cross?

Reader's Response

A Prayer to Complete

Lord, I don't like to talk about death, do You? I'd rather talk about life. But I guess first things first, right, Lord? Help me to die today, so I can truly live this day for You. I specifically desire to live for You today in the area of . . .

Going Deeper

1. What are two modern uses of the cross that distract from the reality of death?
   - (1) _____
   - (2) _____
2. The writer indicates there are two crosses in the New Testament. In what way does your cross compare to Jesus' cross?
   - (1) _____
   - (2) _____
   - (3) _____

(4) _____
3. In what ways is your cross different from the one on which Jesus died?
   (1) _____
   (2) _____
   (3) _____
   (4) _____
4. Make a list of "daily" disciplines that are a part of your life. Contrast it with a list of "daily" disciplines that you would like to be a part of your life.

   Current Daily Disciplines   *Desired Daily Disciplines*
   (1) _____   (1) _____
   (2) _____   (2) _____
   (3) _____   (3) _____
   (4) _____   (4) _____
   (5) _____   (5) _____
5. How are you doing with your cross?

DAY 27 ━━━━━━━━━━━━━━━━ DATE _____
Qualifications for Followship (3)

"If anyone wishes to come after Me, let him . . . follow Me" (Luke 9:23).

Followship is not yet complete when one has denied self and taken one's own cross. One must then do something else. Jesus mentioned a third qualification for followship. This is the one most often forgotten, perhaps because of its simplicity. This one is taken for granted. Jesus said if one wished to come after Him, one should "follow." Simple? Yes! But even when you have denied yourself and taken up your cross, what have you really done? Followship is incomplete until you begin to "follow."

How do I "follow" Jesus? One way is to follow Him in the Word. It is for certain we will find Him there. Daily reading of some portion of the life of Jesus from God's Word will assist in followship. Time out must be taken for this. Even Jesus Himself got away from the crowds and from His disciples in order to understand and follow the will of God more completely. The responsibility to get alone with the Word of God is as much a spiritual discipline as is the responsibility to work in the world.

But one must not stay in isolation. One must also follow Jesus in the world. In a sense the song line "the cross before me, the world behind me" is a true statement. But in another sense, the world is not behind me. The world is around me. Jesus must also be followed as one discovers Him in other persons, in nature, and in human experiences.

Jesus lives in the Word and in the world. In these two places you must find and follow Him. Qualifications for Followship— deny self, take up your cross, and follow Jesus—tough but true!

Reader's Response

A Prayer to Complete

Wow, God, You really laid it on the line, didn't You? I'm not sure I can do it. In fact the more I think about it, the more I know I can't follow You in my own strength. So thanks for sending Jesus into my life to help me. Help me today to really, really "follow" Him especially in . . .

Going Deeper

1. In what sense is followship incomplete until you begin to follow?
2. List two ways you presently follow Jesus in the Word.
   (1) _____
   (2) _____
3. What are two other ways you could follow Jesus in the Word?

(1) _____

(2) _____

4. List two ways you presently follow Jesus in the world.

(1) _____

(2) _____

5. What are two other ways you could follow Jesus in the world?

(1) _____

(2) _____

6. What is one way Jesus helps you to follow Him?

(1) _____

DAY 28 ━━━━━━━━━━━━ DATE _____

The Privileged People of God (1)

"Come." "From every tribe and tongue and people and nation . . . to be a kingdom" (Rev. 6:1,3,5,7; 5:9-10).

Your presence is requested at the coronation of the King. Wow! You have been invited to a coronation ceremony! Four different times in Revelation 6:1-8 the word *come* appears. This simply echoes the words of Jesus in Matthew 25:34: "Then the King will say to those on His right, 'Come, you who are blessed of My Father, inherit the kingdom prepared for you from the foundation of the world,' " and the words of Jesus in Matthew 11:28: "Come to Me all who are weary and heavy-laden." You are among the privileged people of God. You have been invited to the coronation of the King of kings.

But there's more! Not only are you invited to the coronation, but you are part of the immediate family. Revelation 5:9-10 says that Jesus was slain in order to purchase for God a family of people "from every tribe and tongue and people and nation." Paul knew this when he wrote in Romans 8:16-17: "We are children of God, and if children, heirs of God and fellow-heirs with Christ." As a member of God's forever family you will "inherit the kingdom prepared" and, in fact, are now enjoying some of the benefits of inheritance. And again in Galatians 4:7: "You are no longer a slave, but a son; and if a son, then an heir through God."

Reader's Response

A Prayer to Complete

Thank you, Father, for inviting me into Your family and making me an heir of Your kingdom. Help me today to see my fellow Christians as joint heirs as well as fellow family members. Especially help me in my relationship with . . .

Going Deeper

1. When did you first understand your "invitation" to the coronation of the King, and in what way did you respond?
2. Jesus' words in Matthew 11:28 indicate you can continue to come to Him when you are "heavy-laden." List three ways you have been "heavy laden" this month.
   (1) _____
   (2) _____
   (3) _____
3. How have you "come" to Jesus in the above areas (or how do you need to "come" to Jesus)?
   (1) _____
   (2) _____
   (3) _____
4. What does it mean to you to be a part of the "family" of God?
5. The writer indicates that you "are now enjoying some of the benefits of inheritance." List four of these benefits below.
   (1) _____
   (2) _____

(3) _____

(4) _____

DAY 29 ————————————— DATE _____

The Privileged People of God (2)

"Rest for a little while longer, until the number of their fellow servants and their brethren . . . should be completed also" (Rev. 6:11).

Invited to the coronation of the King as a member of the immediate family! Could there possibly be anything more privileged than that? Yes, there can, and there is!

Not only are you invited as a family member, but the coronation will not begin until you get there. In Revelation 6:9-11, the saints of God who are already present with Him are seen as asking when the end of time will come and the coronation begin. They were told to "rest for a little while longer, until the number of their fellow servants and their brethren . . . should be completed."

After listing the "roll call of the faithful" the writer of Hebrews makes a statement in Hebrews 11:39-40, "All these, having gained approval through their faith, did not receive what was promised, because God had provided something better for us, so that apart from us they should not be made perfect." Then he described Jesus as not only the "author" but also the "finisher" (KJV) or "perfector" of our faith (12:2).

There is coming a great Coronation Day when He will be crowned King of kings and Lord of lords. You have been invited because you are a part of the immediate family. But even more privileged are you—it will not begin until after you arrive, and God chooses to "finish" the faith.

Reader's Response

A Prayer to Complete

Father, for Your patience with me I am especially thankful. You have chosen me to be a part of the privileged people. You await my presence even as I await and experience Your presence. Make me aware right now that privilege brings with it responsibility. May I see responsibility today in . . .

Going Deeper

1. What is your reaction to the fact that the coronation of the King will not begin until after you arrive?
2. Do you know someone who has already gone on to heaven? In what way did they deserve to hear God say, "Rest for a little while longer"?
3. Of what significance is it to you that Jesus is the "author" of your life?
4. List three ways that Jesus is "perfecting" your life.
   (1) _____
   (2) _____
   (3) _____
5. How is your experience with Jesus today a foretaste of how you expect to experience Him in heaven?

DAY 30 ───────────────── DATE ─────────────

The Responsible People of God (1)

"Present your bodies a living and holy sacrifice, acceptable to God, which is your spiritual service" (Rom. 12:1).

Privilege brings with it a corresponding responsibility. We are the privileged people of God. We are also the responsible people of God. We have first priority responsibility to God Himself.

Paul begged those to whom he wrote "by the mercies of God" to make a presentation of themselves, their bodies to God. If I present my body, I present all that I am: physical, mental, emotional, and spiritual. It is a 100 percent gift. I may tithe 10 percent of my possessions, but I am to give 100 percent of myself.

Paul leaned back on his Old Testament training to write about this presentation being a "living sacrifice." This was in contrast to the sacrifice of dead animals in Old Testament times. Also the presentation was to be a "holy sacrifice." A sacrifice that is "living and holy" will be "acceptable to God."

In a world where so many ideas and organizations beckon for our allegiance, why should you give yourself 100 percent to God? Paul said that it is the only reasonable thing you can do. In light of the fact that Jesus Christ, who in the beginning clothed the valleys and fields, was allowed to hang naked on the cross, it is your "reasonable service" (KJV). In light of the fact that Jesus, who claimed to be the Water of life, was allowed to cry "I thirst" on the cross, it is your "reasonable service." In light of the fact that Jesus, who said, "I am the life," died on the cross, it is your "reasonable service." You are responsible for living in right relationship with God. And that makes sense.

Reader's Response

A Prayer to Complete
Thank you, God, for being all I need You to be. May I find it "reasonable" to live in right relationship with You. Today I need to experience that right relationship in . . .

Going Deeper

1. Since Paul indicated we are to present our all to God, list one item in each of the following areas that you need to present to God or an item on which you need prayer in each area.
   (1) Physical _____
   (2) Mental _____
   (3) Emotional _____
   (4) Spiritual _____

2. Out of your experiences, list three reasons why it is "reasonable" for you to serve God.
   (1) _____
   (2) _____
   (3) _____

3. How would you define "living and holy sacrifice" as it relates to your sacrifice to God?

4. The writer began this reading with the statement, "Privilege brings with it a corresponding responsibility." Below list three "privileges" which are yours with the "corresponding responsibility."

Privileges	*Responsibilities*
(1) _____	_____
(2) _____	_____
(3) _____	_____

DAY 31 ——————————— DATE _____

The Responsible People of God (2)

"Do not be conformed to this world, but be transformed by the renewing of your mind, that you may prove what the will of God is" (Rom. 12:2).

Being one of the privileged people of God does not allow you the freedom to live in isolation, nor does it allow you to spend all your time working on your relationships with God. Being one of the privileged people of God brings with it the responsibility to be rightly related to the world around you.

One of the strongest temptations you face is the temptation to be like the people around you. You want to identify with your peers. No one enjoys being "different." Some have learned to live with being "different," but no one enjoys it. Paul said, "Do not be conformed to this world." You need to be very careful at this point lest you overemphasize or underemphasize this. Remember that Paul is writing about your responsibility to the world around you.

You ought to be thankful for the word *but* in this verse. Before you get hung up on conformity, you must read the *but*. "But be transformed." Here is the key. The relationship is inward, not outward. You are "different" on the inside because you have been and are being "transformed" by the renewing of your mind. Take care of the inside first. Once that is settled you will not worry so much about outward conformity.

Having worked at rightly relating yourself to God and to the world around you, you will "prove" the will of God. The will of God for your life will not often be found as you search for it, but it will be found as you rightly relate yourself in a responsible way to God and to others. How awesome to be one of the responsible people of God!

Reader's Response

A Prayer to Complete
Lord, down deep I want to be rightly related to others. Help me to be more concerned with inner transformation than with outward conformity. My struggle today is related to . . .

Going Deeper
1. In twenty-five words or less describe the "world around you."

_____

_____

_____

2. List three ways in which you are similar to your peers.
   (1) _____
   (2) _____
   (3) _____
3. List three ways in which you are different from your peers.
   (1) _____
   (2) _____
   (3) _____
4. How can you balance the positive peer pressure in your life with the challenge to "not be conformed to this world"?
5. The writer said, "The will of God for your life will not often be found as you search for it, but it will be found as you rightly relate yourself in a responsible way to God and to others." If this is true, how will you discover God's will for your life for the remainder of your hundred days of service?

DAY 32 ━━━━━━━━━━━━━ DATE _____
The Responsible People of God (3)

"For I say, through the grace given unto me, to every man that is among you, not to think of himself more highly than he ought to think; but to think soberly, according as God hath dealt to every man the measure of faith" (Rom. 12:3, KJV).

You have a responsibility to God as a believer. You also have a responsibility to those around you. Being one of the privileged people of God allows you to live and minister within these two relationships. It also prevents you from stopping with just these two. To balance your Christian life you must also be rightly related to yourself.

Paul begins with the negative side by encouraging you to not think more highly of yourself than you ought to think. Being a Christian servant and especially a leader among peers might tend to lead to those kinds of thoughts. He could just as easily have said (and, in fact, may have implied) that you are not to think more lowly of yourself than you ought to think. Long, hard days of service with little visible results might tend to lead to these kinds of thoughts.

The positive side of the verse brings the relationship to self into proper perspective. Paul encourages you to "think soberly" or balanced. Think sober thoughts like the privilege of servanthood. Think sober thoughts like the responsibility of servanthood. God has allotted to each a measure of faith, so think sober, responsible thoughts about your relationship to yourself.

Reader's Response

A Prayer to Complete

Lord, I want to know who I am and to be able to think sober thoughts about myself. Guide me to a balanced understanding of myself and a proper application of those thoughts as I work and minister today. Especially guide my thoughts during
. . .

Going Deeper

1. List five descriptive words about yourself at this point in your life.
    (1) _____
    (2) _____
    (3) _____
    (4) _____
    (5) _____
2. Evaluate each of the above self-descriptions. Ask your Christian friends to make a list or comment on your list. Are you thinking too highly of yourself? Scratch out the descriptions that are too "high."
3. Now evaluate from the "low" perspective. Compare your

list to that of your Christian friends. Are you describing yourself more lowly than you ought? Scratch out the descriptions that are too "low."

4. On the scale below mark with an X the "measure" or level of your faith at the beginning of this book. Then mark with an X your measure of faith now. What does the difference tell you?

No faith   Fully matured faith

|——|——|——|——|——|——|——|——|——|

5. List two "sober" or "balanced" conclusions about yourself.

(1) _____

(2) _____

DAY 33 ——————————————— DATE _____

Investments (1)

"The grass withers, the flower fades,/But the word of our God stands forever" (Isa. 40:8).

The faithful follower of Jesus Christ, who in the process of self-denial plugs into God's power, begins naturally to look for ways to invest himself. Followship or discipleship that is not invested or applied is not Christian followship or discipleship. Followers of Jesus may invest themselves in many ways. One way that pays eternal dividends is to invest in the Word of God. In fact, Scripture is the main place where one can be absolutely sure that one is communicating with God.

So God's Word must be read. Paul challenged Timothy to "give attention to the . . . reading of Scripture" (1 Tim. 4:13). In addition to reading it, one must also study God's Word. Second Timothy 2:15 says, "Study to shew thyself approved unto God" (KJV). Like the people of Berea, we should receive "the word with great eagerness, examining the Scriptures daily" (Acts 17:11).

Further, one must meditate on God's Word. The psalmist

said, "Let the . . . meditation of my heart/Be acceptable in Thy sight" (Ps. 19:14). Often, our Lord went out early in the morning to be alone with the Father; it was before daylight, thus forcing Him to meditate with no light by which to read or study (Mark 1:35). Also, one needs to memorize portions of God's Word. Like the psalmist, Scripture should be "treasured" in the heart (Ps. 119:11). Jesus quoted Scripture at His temptation and also from the cross.

Finally, one must do it. Perhaps most important of all, there must be application of what you read, study, meditate on, and memorize. James 1:22 encourages being "doers of the word." Hebrews 5:13-14 indicates that one moves from "milk" to "solid food" when one applies or puts into "practice" the "milk." The Word of God is an eternal investment.

Reader's Response

A Prayer to Complete

Lord, like the psalmist I wish to keep my way pure "by keeping it according to Thy Word" (Ps. 119:9). Help me today to make proper investment in Your Word as follows . . .

Going Deeper

1. Write a one-sentence definition of discipleship.

   _____

   _____

2. Does your definition of discipleship include the idea of application or putting the theory into practice? If not, rewrite your sentence definition to include application.

   _____

   _____

3. List one way you have been investing in the Word of God during these hundred days in the following areas.
   (1) Reading Scripture _____
   (2) Studying Scripture _____

(3) Meditating on Scripture_____

(4) Memorizing Scripture_____

(5) Applying Scripture _____

4. In which of the above areas are you the weakest? What is one action you could take that would increase your investment in that area?

_____

_____

5. Check the food that most often describes your spiritual diet.

____ Milk   ____ Low-calorie diet

____ Baby food   ____ Water

____ Liquid diet   ____ Solid food

____ Junk food

6. What could be done this month to balance your spiritual diet?

DAY 34 ————————— DATE _____

Investments (2)

"An hour is coming, in which all . . . shall hear His voice, and shall come forth . . . to a resurrection" (John 5:28-29).

If one is looking to invest material possessions, one will search out what appears to be a sure thing—one that will pay dividends. Likewise is it with spiritual possessions. Thus spiritual possessions should be invested not only in the Word of God which "stands forever" (Isa. 40:8) but in persons whose souls are eternal.

You should invest in the people of God in the world. Not all of God's creatures are in Christ. Some are in and of this world. In fulfillment of His Great Commission, you must see that these are discipled as you go among them. Jesus said, "I, if I be lifted up from the earth, will draw all men to Myself" (John 12:32). As you go in a love relationship with His people who are in the world, lift Him up. Jesus then draws persons to Himself. You do not make disciples. You lift up Jesus. He makes disciples.

You should also invest yourself in the people of God who are in Christ. Ephesians 4:11-16 indicates that each of us has been given a particular assignment or calling, but all of us as believers are to be "building up . . . the body of Christ" (v. 12). It is this "body of Christ" that He is interested in presenting to Himself, "the church in all her glory, having no spot or wrinkle or any such thing; but that she should be holy and blameless (5:27)." Christ loved these people—indeed, loves us—so much that He died for the church. You can at least invest your life in the people who are in Christ and who are triumphant.

But take warning. Investments in the lives of people are risky. You will sometimes get hurt. Investments take time. You will grow weary waiting. But Jesus is our example. He invested His life in people. We are to be imitators of Him.

Reader's Response

A Prayer to Complete

People are difficult, Lord. It's hard to invest in the lives of some people I know. Help me today to be a good steward of what I have been given by passing it on to some of your people whether I like them or not. I might look for that person in
. . .

Going Deeper

1. List five persons in whom you have made the largest time investment during these hundred days of servanthood.

    (1) _____

    (2) _____

    (3) _____

    (4) _____

72

(5) _____

2. Which of these persons are non-Christians. Which are Christians? Is your time investment in persons well balanced?
3. Describe your particular career calling from God.
4. How can your calling be used in "building up . . . the body of Christ" (Eph. 4:11-16)?
5. React to the statement: "Investments in the lives of persons are risky."
6. List three risks that you have taken during these hundred days related to investment in the lives of persons. What has been the results of these investments?

(1) _____
(2) _____
(3) _____

DAY 35 ━━━━━━━━━━ DATE _____
'Round but Right

"God did not lead them by the way of the land of the Philistines, even though it was near. . . . Hence God led the people around by the way of the wilderness" (Ex. 13:17-18).

After all the children of Israel had been through in Egypt, you know they had to be in a hurry to get on to the Promised Land. They were to learn, perhaps the hard way, that God's time schedule is different from ours. God knew best.

A shortcut to the Promised Land promised only war in the territory of the Philistines. In all probability, the children of Israel would have turned back to Egypt. Their faith would not have been strong enough to make it through (Ex. 13:17).

In addition to not being prepared for the potentialities of the shortcut, they needed the disciplines of the desert. They needed to hear and learn the Law. They needed to learn how to govern themselves. The musician and the athlete have learned by experience that there is no shortcut for discipline. There is a price to be paid for success. It was not so much the purpose of God to give the children of Israel the Promised Land as it was His purpose to make them worthy to possess it.

So the journey that could have been made in ten days following the straight trade route from Egypt to Canaan lasted for forty years. In this case, the long road was the better road.

As we get anxious in our own ministry and desire to get on to the "promise," we need to remember that sometimes God leads 'round, but always God leads right.

Reader's Response

A Prayer to Complete

God, forgive my hurry to get things done. Slow me down to the place where I can understand Your timing. May You and I go forward today in pace with each other. In order to keep pace with You I need to . . .

Going Deeper

1. From the Scripture passages list some of the things the "children of Israel had been through in Egypt" that caused them to be in a hurry to reach the Promised Land.
   (1) Exodus 1:8-14 _____
   (2) Exodus 1:15-16 _____
   (3) Exodus 5:4-9 _____
2. What are three things which make you impatient?
   (1) _____
   (2) _____
   (3) _____
3. Can you see how these hundred days are a part of God's perfect timing? What would have been some of the results had you been where you are today five years ago?
4. What are some disciplines that God has taught you during

74

these hundred days that will make you better prepared for the future?

(1) _____
(2) _____
(3) _____
(4) _____

5. The writer said, "There is a price to be paid for success." What is the price paid for any success which you have experienced during these hundred days?

DAY 36 ———————————— DATE _____
Perspectives on Love

"Let us love one another, for love is from God." (1 John 4:7).

Do you remember when you received your first kaleidoscope? Remember how fascinated you were as you looked through the opening and watched the ingredients move to form new and exciting formations? It seemed that there were at least a thousand different formations. Although you probably did not think about it at the time, the ingredients in the kaleidoscope never changed. Your perspective is what changed as the ingredients moved about.

Love is like that! The ingredients never change, but your perspective changes. Your childhood perspective on love has changed. Your present perspective on love is changing. Love means many things to many different people. Your perspective on love is affected by your age, environment, education, personality, beliefs, and a lot of other factors. It matters not where you are—geographically, emotionally, spiritually, mentally, or chronologically—one fact never changes: "God is love, and the one who abides in love abides in God, and God abides in him" (1 John 4:16).

Four times in 1 John 4:7-21 John referred to perfect love or love being perfected. What is perfect love? Only as you see and experience love in all its proper perspectives can you begin to understand perfect love. And you cannot begin to see and experience the proper perspectives until you understand the unchanging ingredients: "God is love" (1 John 4:8).

Reader's Response

A Prayer to Complete

God, as I focus on You, may I experience love in all its proper perspectives. Thank You for loving me. Lord, I really want to express my love for You and for others today. May I be sensitive to avenues for expression of that love through . . .

Going Deeper

1. How would you define "love"?
2. What light does 1 John 4:7 shed on your definition of love?
3. Since "God is love" what are three characteristics of "perfect love"?
   (1) _____
   (2) _____
   (3) _____
4. What is one way you have experienced "perfect love" during these hundred days of servanthood?

DAY 37 ───────────────── DATE _____
Perspectives on Love: God Loves You

"Love is from God; . . . not that we loved God, but that He loved us . . . God is love, . . . He first loved us" (1 John 4:7,10,16,19).

Take up your mental kaleidoscope and look at the unchanging ingredients of love. The first perspective you see is God's love for His creatures. God has always loved us. We read of

Jesus saying that He was loved by the Father "before the foundation of the world" (John 17:24). Did you realize that before God ever created anything He loved! That means that at the very core of all that exists is love. There has never been a time when God did not love you, and He loves you today.

God loves all people equally. Some know more about God's love than others. Some can appropriate God's love better than others. Some can share God's love more effectively than others. But no one person has more of God's love than another person. The Bible teaches over and over that God loves all human beings totally. He gave his Son for *all* people. His commission to His followers was and is to share this love with "all nations." God loves you today as much as He has ever loved anyone.

God will always love humanity. Paul asked: "Who shall separate us from the love of Christ?" After listing such possibilities as tribulation, distress, persecution, famine, nakedness, peril, sword, life, death, angels, principalities, powers, things present, and things to come, he argued that nothing can "separate us from the love of God" (Rom. 8:35-39, KJV). No matter who you really are right now, or where you ever go, God will always love you, and for some it will come as a comfort that "He will be quiet in His love" (Zeph. 3:17).

Reader's Response

A Prayer to Complete

God, thank You for loving me before I existed. Thank You for loving me as much as you've ever loved anyone. Thank You for the promise to always love me. Teach me today that You love me in spite of my . . .

Going Deeper

1. List three ways you have experienced God's love for you during these hundred days of servanthood.

   (1) _____

(2) _____

(3) _____

2. What are two implications of the fact that God loved Jesus "before the foundation of the world" (John 17:24)?

(1) _____

(2) _____

3. How do you react to the statement, "God loves all people equally"? What does this mean if applied to your situation?

4. List three reasons why God *should* love you.

(1) _____

(2) _____

(3) _____

5. What does your answer to the above question tell you about God's love to you?

DAY 38 ───────────────── DATE _____

Perspective on Love: You Love God

"The one who loves God" (1 John 4:21).

Again, take up your mental kaleidoscope and look at the unchanging ingredients of love. The first perspective seen was that God loves you. Now, the second perspective on love to be seen is that you love God. The deadest thing in this world is a one-way love. This is true on the human level, and it is certainly true on a divine level. The most natural thing to do when loved is to return that love. God loves you and expects you to return that love.

Caution! When God loved you, it cost Him. It cost Him the life of His only Son. Now, when you choose to return God's love, it will cost you. In the midst of the age-old talk of "free love," God's kind of love has never been free. Granted, it cost you nothing to accept God's love—He paid that cost. But once you begin to apply His love, it ceases to be free. Returning

God's love will cost you at the point of service and investment in the lives of His people.

Jesus taught Peter that if he loved Him, Peter was to serve or "Tend My sheep" (John 21:17). You will learn that love and service are interlocked. You may serve without love, but you cannot properly love without serving. And that means serving all kinds of "sheep." The disciples learned early that Jesus had "other sheep which are not of this fold" (John 10:16). You will learn as you serve that He has some sheep you don't particularly like. Keep your eyes fixed on Him. It is because He loves that we serve. Hear His voice amidst all other voices saying, "Do you love Me?" . . . "Tend My sheep."

Reader's Response

A Prayer to Complete

God, I really want to love You. Sometimes I wish I could love just You and not people. Sometimes people are so unlovely. Teach me that if I really love You I must be willing to pay the cost of service. Help me today in my service to . . .

Going Deeper
1. List four ways you have shown your love for God during these hundred days of servanthood.
    (1) _____
    (2) _____
    (3) _____
    (4) _____
2. React to the statement: "The deadest thing in this world is a one-way love."
3. What has it cost you to love God during these hundred days?
4. List three persons in whom you have invested time during these hundred days. How could you serve God better through your investment in the lives of these persons?

(1) _____

(2) _____

(3) _____

5. Have you met any "sheep" you don't like? How can you follow Jesus' instructions to "Tend my sheep" with this unliked "sheep"?

Perspective on Love: Let Us Love Each Other

"Let us love one another. . . . We also ought to love one another. . . . The one who loves God should love his brother also" (1 John 4:7,11,21).

Once more, take up your mental kaleidoscope and look at the unchanging ingredients of love. Remember the first perspective was one of God's love to man. The second was man's love to God which involves service. Now, the third perspective and perhaps the most crucial is the one that says, "Let us love each other." It is easy to say that we feel God's love for us; and it's easy to say that we love God in return. It is even possible to convince some that we love God enough to serve Him. But now it gets tough.

John said, "If someone says, 'I love God,' and hates his brother, he is a liar" (1 John 4:20). Love lives and breathes at the level of brotherhood. Do you have any brothers or sisters in God's family whom you hate? Or even dislike? John indicates that if your answer is yes, you ought to stop claiming that you love God. You are lying. "The one who does not love his brother whom he has seen, cannot love God whom he has not seen" (1 John 4:20). How long has it been since you openly and honestly expressed love for a brother or sister?

What was it that continually amazed those who observed the New Testament church? Did they admire their preaching? Or their faithfulness? Or their accomplishments? The thing that amazed the observers was how these followers of Jesus could love each other. Diverse of character, they stopped looking at each other long enough to look together at Jesus. May *their* number increase! It is only as we look together at Him that we can properly love each other.

Reader's Response

A Prayer to Complete

God, I confess that sometimes I'd rather look at You than others. I pray that having looked at You I might look now upon all persons with love. May I be aware of opportunities today to openly and honestly express my love for . . .

Going Deeper

1. List three ways you have loved others during these hundred days.

   (1) _____
   (2) _____
   (3) _____

2. Since "We love, because He first loved us" (1 John 4:19), what changes, if any, should you make in the way you have attempted to love persons?

3. What is one way that you should join your fellow Christians in looking "together at Jesus"?

4. React to the statement, "It is only as we look together at Him that we can properly love each other."

5. Name two persons you ought to attempt to love during the next few days. What will it take to love them?

   (1) _____
   (2) _____

DAY 40 ——————————— DATE ——————————

Perspectives on Love: Perfect Love

"His love is perfected in us. . . . By this, love is perfected. . . . Perfect love casts out fear. . . . The one who fears is not perfected in love" (1 John 4:12,17-18).

Set down your mental kaleidoscope and learn a lesson about love when it is made perfect. Perfect love is experienced from three different perspectives. The first perspective is that God loves you. He always has. He loves you as much as He loves anyone. He always will love you. The second perspective on love is that you love God. To return God's love is natural, but it is costly. It will cost you in the area of service. The third perspective on love is that we ought to love each other. If we don't love each other, then we don't love God. The disciples succeeded largely because they learned to translate God's love to each other. Only as you see and experience love in all its proper perspectives can you begin to understand perfect love, and you cannot begin to see and experience the proper perspectives until you understand the unchanging ingredients: "God is love" (1 John 4:8).

"See how great a love the Father has bestowed upon us, that we should be called children of God; and such we are" (1 John 3:1). Rejoice, child of God! You are the recipient of the greatest of all gifts from the greatest of all gift givers: God gives you love. And His kind of love, "so amazing, so divine,/Demands my soul, my life, my all."

Reader's Response

A Prayer to Complete

God, thank You that Your love is perfect. As I grow and learn, may I understand more and more of Your love. Today I need to understand and apply . . .

Going Deeper
1. Rewrite the definition of love which you wrote on Day 36.
2. What differences appear in your new definition?
3. List any new thoughts you've had about love this week.
   (1) _____
   (2) _____
   (3) _____
   (4) _____
4. What did John mean when he wrote, "God is love" (1 John 4:8)?
5. If love really does demand "soul . . . life . . . all," what does it specifically demand from you?
   (1) _____
   (2) _____

DAY 41 ——————————————— DATE ——————————
Life in the Now

"For now we really live" (1 Thess. 3:8).

Many persons fall into the trap of avoiding the "now" while living in either the past or the future. Oh, there is excitement in the "now," and there is adventure and risk and pleasure in the "now," but to deal seriously with "now" is unheard of for many.

Yesterday was so good, some refuse to move on. Yesterday was so bad, others are afraid to move on. In the Bible, when God's people grew complacent in worshiping the past, they got a stern "move on" from God. There is great value in the past, but God's people were not meant to live there.

Tomorrow may be so attractive, some rush past the good present to get there. Tomorrow may be so hopeful that others would rather dwell there than in their hopelessness of today. When God's people spent too much time worshiping the future, they got a gentle reminder of the importance of the now.

Although there is value in the future, we are not to get there before our time.

If you fail to learn from yesterday, the chances are you will not live to your fullest today. If you have no hope for a better tomorrow, chances are you are settling for less today. But the real truth is, if you are not enjoying the "now," you won't enjoy tomorrow. Eternity is a continual "now" where we will never have a yesterday or a tomorrow.

So get on with life. Learn from your past and hope for your future, but live in the reality of today.

Reader's Response

A Prayer to Complete

Thank You, God, for the blessings of yesterday and the hope of tomorrow. Help me put them in proper perspective as I live today for You. I need Your special help with . . .

Going Deeper

1. What are two reasons why you might be tempted to stay with the experiences of yesterday (your past)?
   (1) _____
   (2) _____
2. What are two reasons why you might be tempted to hurry into tomorrow (your future)?
   (1) _____
   (2) _____
3. What have you learned from your yesterdays that makes the future brighter and today more meaningful?
   (1) _____
   (2) _____
4. React to the statement, "Eternity is a continual 'now' where we will never have a yesterday or a tomorrow."
5. What could you do today to help someone else enjoy the "reality of today"?

DAY 42 ————————————— DATE ———————————
Daily Routine (1)

"Our inner man is being renewed day by day" (2 Cor. 4:16).

A man once said in my presence, "The trouble with life is that it's so routine." God-sized visions and mountain-moving type faith are both exciting and attention getting. The daily routine is just as exciting.

The daily routine of the disciple of Jesus quite obviously involves relationships with other persons. There are those relationships within the family of God. To miss these is to miss the fellowship, the *koinonia,* of the Christian faith. One of the saddest verses in the New Testament is John 20:24, "But Thomas, one of the twelve, called Didymus, was not with them when Jesus came." The resurrected Lord appeared to His disciples as they met together. But where was Thomas? Somewhere in the night Thomas was trying to make it alone, unaware that the Christian life is to be lived in relationship to other Christians. Thomas missed the fellowship as well as the presence of Jesus. How many times lately have you missed the presence of Jesus because you chose to miss the fellowship of other Christians? First Corinthians 12:13 speaks clearly of these relationships.

There are also to be relationships with non-Christians. Jesus spoke of this on two significant occasions. In the Sermon on the Mount, he said to "love your enemies" (Matt. 5:44), and in the Great Commission, He commanded disciples to "Go therefore and make disciples of all the nations" (Matt. 28:19).

This daily routine becomes exciting as it is lived in relationship both to fellow Christians and to non-Christians. This is the way our Lord intended daily routine to be.

Reader's Response

A Prayer to Complete

God of relationships, assist me today as I try to relate properly to my Christian brothers and sisters and especially as I relate

to those who have yet to accept You as Savior and Lord. I pray
for my relationship with . . .

Going Deeper

1. List three evidences that your "inner man is being renewed
   day by day" (2 Cor. 4:16).

   (1) _____

   (2) _____

   (3) _____

2. In 2 Corinthians 4:18, Paul indicated renewal comes as we
   look "at the things which are not seen; for the things which
   are seen are temporal, but the things which are not seen are
   eternal." What are two of the unseen things which, if you
   looked at them, would bring renewal to you today?

   (1) _____

   (2) _____

3. What does 1 Corinthians 12:13 say concerning the fellowship of Christians?

4. What are two ways you could "love your enemies" (Matt.
   5:44) today?

   (1) _____

   (2) _____

5. What is one human relationship which brings daily renewal
   to you? Thank God right now for this relationship. If you
   could list none, what steps could you take to develop that
   kind of renewing relationship?

DAY 43 ——————————————— DATE _____
Daily Routine (2)

"Our inner man is being renewed day by day" (2 Cor. 4:16).

Not only is your daily routine to be lived in relationship to
other persons—Christians and non-Christians, but it is to be

lived in relationship to God. How does one relate on a daily basis to God? Several suggestions may prove helpful.

There should be a relationship to God through prayer. First Thessalonians 5:17 says to "pray without ceasing." Surely this would involve a daily routine of prayer. Epaphras, an acquaintance of Paul, was said to be "always laboring earnestly for you in his prayers" (Col. 4:12). Jesus said, *"When* you pray" not "if you pray." He assumed disciples would pray.

There should be a relationship to God through the reading, meditating, memorizing, and studying of His Word, the Bible. First Timothy 4:13 says, "Until I come, give attention to the public reading of Scripture." Colossians 3:16 says, "Let the word of Christ dwell in you richly" (KJV). First Timothy 4:15 says, "Meditate upon these things" (KJV). "Study to shew thyself approved unto God" (2 Tim. 2:15, KJV). As surely as there is a time in your daily routine for prayer, there should be a time for a relationship to God through His Word.

One other relationship to God needs to be considered, and that is at the point of availability. Romans 12:1 exhorts us to "present your bodies a living sacrifice, holy, acceptable unto God (KJV). For many, this is a daily routine as they continually find themselves crawling off the altar of sacrifice. Most disciples need to make a daily presentation of their lives to God.

With proper relationship to other persons and proper relationship to God, the daily routine proves to be an exciting venture.

Reader's Response

A Prayer to Complete

Lord, somehow it seems easier to pray when I meet You in a "mountaintop" experience. Praying in the daily routine seems more difficult. Help me to see You today as the God of every day. May today's routine be exciting because of my relationship to You and because of . . .

Going Deeper

1. How does prayer strengthen your relationship with God?
2. How do the following actions strengthen your relationship to God?
   (1) Reading Scripture _____
   (2) Meditating on Scripture_____
   (3) Memorizing Scripture_____
   (4) Studying Scripture _____
3. In what ways do you find yourself "crawling off the altar of sacrifice"?
   (1) _____
   (2) _____
   (3) _____
4. On the scale below, mark with an X your present relationship with God. With an X mark your desired relationship with God by the end of your hundred days of servanthood.

Casual acquaintance   Fully matured

|———|———|———|———|———|———|———|———|———|

5. What are two actions you could take to assist your movement from X to X?
   (1) _____
   (2) _____

DAY 44 ——————————— DATE _____

The Necessity of Fellowship

"But Thomas, one of the twelve, . . . was not with them when Jesus came" (John 20:24).

Where was Thomas? Ten of the twelve disciples were there. It was Sunday night and there was rumor that Jesus was going to be there. That in itself was enough to draw a crowd because He had been killed and buried the preceding Friday. "But Thomas, one of the twelve, . . . was not with them when Jesus came" (John 20:24).

Where was Thomas? Was he out by the fishing boats trying to put the pieces of his life back together? Was he out on the Mount of Olives replaying those last memories of Jesus? Was he wandering the streets of Jerusalem hoping this was all a bad dream? Or was he just alone—trying to make it by himself? We do not know where Thomas was, but we know what he missed by not being with the group.

Thomas missed the fellowship that can come only from within the family of believers. There is strength in fellowship. There is encouragement in fellowship. There is newfound joy in fellowship. There is rediscovered meaning in fellowship. More than all, there is the presence of Jesus in this kind of family fellowship. And Thomas missed it. Did he find any of these things apart from the fellowship? And even if he did, what did he substitute for the value of sharing his discovery? What could he substitute for missing the resurrected Christ?

No doubt you have had those times when you need to get away. That's OK. There is a bit of Thomas in us all. Sometimes we even need to go off and ask questions. But Thomas came back! You will also. The price tag of trying to go it alone in the pilgrimage is too high. Just ask Judas.

Reader's Response

A Prayer to Complete

Lord, give me those times to be alone and think, but bring me quickly back to the fellowship. Help me today to sense the strength and joy of Christian friends as I serve. Among my Christian friends I am especially thankful for . . .

Going Deeper

1. If you had been Thomas, knowing Jesus had been crucified, where would you have gone?
   ____ To the fishing boat
   ____ To visit friends

_____ To be alone
_____ To get lost in a crowd
_____ Other

2. When you are away from the fellowship of God's people, where do you go?

3. By missing the fellowship, Thomas missed a lot. What do you miss by being away from your Christian group when you are away?
   (1) _____
   (2) _____
   (3) _____

4. What do you uniquely gain from new fellowships of believers in which you find yourself on occasion?
   (1) _____
   (2) _____
   (3) _____

5. Having been part of at least two different fellowships, what are some common characteristics of the people of God when they gather together?
   (1) _____
   (2) _____
   (3) _____
   (4) _____

6. What is the "price tag of trying to go it alone in the pilgrimage" for you?

DAY 45 ━━━━━━━━━━━━ DATE _____
The Winning Team

"You will not be able to overthrow them" (Acts 5:39).

The Jewish religious leaders were in a dilemma. Hating the Christians and all who identified with Christians, they had tried to stop them. They killed the Leader. But the attempt to keep Him in the grave was as futile as if they had tried to prevent the morning sun from dawning or the evening shadows from gathering.

Failing there, these opponents of Christianity had put the followers of Jesus in jail, but angels let them out. When they put Christians in prison, Christians prayed down the walls or prayed open the doors. When they whipped Christians, Christians departed singing and rejoicing to be found worthy to suffer for Jesus. These fearless fishermen and their peers were not afraid of threats or prisons or stripes or death. What could the Jews do? It was during yet another attempt to stop the movement of Christianity that they heard their answer.

"Gamaliel, a teacher of the Law, respected by all the people" (Acts 5:34), and probably Paul's teacher, said on this occasion one of the smartest things that has ever been said about religious movements. Gamaliel said of Christians, "Stay away from these men and let them alone, for if this plan or action should be of men, it will be overthrown; but if it is of God, you will not be able to overthrow them; or else you may even be found fighting against God" (Acts 5:38-39).

What does this mean to you? To me it means first that when persecuted for your Christianity, you stand in an honorable line of people stretching back into the Book of Acts. It also means that your belief has stood the test of time. Those who have fought have indeed found themselves "fighting against God." You're on the winning team. Celebrate victory today!

Reader's Response

A Prayer to Complete

Thank You, God, for my Christian heritage. Make me worthy to be a part of this winning team. In the midst of today's battles may I remember to celebrate victory especially in the area of . . .

Going Deeper

1. Gamaliel compared the movement begun by Jesus to movements begun by two other men. Name these other men.
   (1) Acts 5:36 _____
   (2) Acts 5:37 _____
2. What was the result of their movements?
   (1) _____
   (2) _____
3. How was the movement begun by Jesus different from the two examples used by Gamaliel?
   (1) _____
   (2) _____
   (3) _____
4. What does it mean to you personally to be on the winning team?
5. How can you "Celebrate victory today"?

DAY 46 ━━━━━━━━━━━━━━━ DATE _____

Becoming Sensitive to Missed Opportunities

   "And they marveled" (John 4:27).

   While Jesus waited at the wellside near Sychar, the disciples went into the city to buy food. Presently, a woman came to draw water from the well, and there took place an encounter between Jesus and the Samaritan woman (the woman at the well). This encounter resulted in Jesus' going to her town, and "many of the Samaritans believed on Him" (John 4:39).

   Two things are extremely interesting because the facts are not in the recorded story. In John 4:27 we are told that the disciples "marveled" that Jesus was speaking to the woman. They were surprised that she was there. Is it not possible that on their way into Sychar they had passed the woman on her way to the well? If they did, it's reasonable that the disciples did not notice her much less attempt to minister to her. After all, these disciples were on their way to buy food for Jesus.

In John 4:39 we are told that many Samaritans believed, "because of the word of the woman." What about the word of the disciples? Were they not in town for some time as they bought food? Is it possible that they did not bear testimony for Jesus while they were in town?

We bear witness well while we are in the spotlight, but when we are no longer in the spotlight, we sometimes forget our responsibility. How is your witness out of the spotlight? How do you live when you are in a place where no one knows you? Who are you when you're not on mission?

Like the disciples, our purpose is pure. We are attempting to do something for Jesus. But also like the disciples, we sometimes overlook or neglect our ministry in the midst of our ministry. Christian witness is a full-time calling.

Reader's Response

A Prayer to Complete

Lord, make me sensitive to areas of ministry out of the mainstream and help me be full-time in my commitment to You today. Make me sensitive to . . .

Going Deeper
1. From what you know of this story (John 4:1-42), why do you think the disciples "marveled" at the fact that Jesus was talking with the woman?
2. Can you find two reasons in this story why the people of Sychar believed in Jesus?
   (1) _____
   (2) _____
3. Is there a recent experience (perhaps this week) where you overlooked someone in need? What do you think would

have been the result had you stopped to minister to that need?

4. Respond to the statement, "We sometimes overlook or neglect our ministry in the midst of our ministry."
5. How would you answer the question, "Who are you when you're not on mission?"
6. What is one thing you could do today or tomorrow that would make you more sensitive to opportunities for ministry?

DAY 47 ━━━━━━━━━━ DATE _____
Results of a New Vision of God

"Then Moses went up with Aaron, Nadab and Abihu, and seventy of the elders of Israel" (Ex. 24:9-10).

They were confused. These leaders of Israel had been called out, but now their marching orders were muddled. No new nation yet existed. The Promised Land was still a dream. The people were unsure. Yet these leaders "saw the God of Israel" (Ex. 24:10).

Many times, when our circumstances begin to get the best of us, we find ourselves needing a fresh vision of God. In the case of Moses and his fellow leaders, this vision resulted in several things.

The first result of this fresh vision was a new understanding of God. They had recently experienced the wrath of God as well as the distrust of their followers. Now they experienced a communication based on love and trust rather than fear and uncertainty. The Bible says that God "did not stretch out His hand against the nobles of the sons of Israel" (Ex. 24:11).

The second result of this fresh vision was a new relationship between themselves. So at peace were they with each other that "they ate and drank" (Ex. 24:11). One is usually at peace with one's peers when one can eat and drink with them. Seemingly, a new vision of God always leads to a deeper fellowship of the faithful.

The third result of this fresh vision was the entering into of a new covenant. In those days, the meal confirmed the covenant. So in fellowship were they with God and with each other, that they responded, "All that the Lord has spoken we will do, and we will be obedient!" (Ex. 24:7).

In the midst of our most trying times, let us seek a new vision of God.

Reader's Response

A Prayer to Complete

God, give us a new vision of You and having seen You again may we focus with freshness upon each other, upon ourselves, and upon our ministry. More than anywhere else, I need to see a new vision of You in . . .

Going Deeper

1. What bold statement had the people made (Ex. 24:7) to Moses preceeding this new vision of God?
2. Do you think there is any significance to the fact that the attitude reflected in this statement preceeded the new vision of God? If so, what was the significance?
3. What are two new understandings of God you have discovered during your hundred days of servanthood?
   (1) _____
   (2) _____
4. Has your vision of God deepened your relationship with your peers? If so, how?
5. What is one action and one attitude that could enable you to have a fresh vision of God?
   (1) Action: _____
   (2) Attitude: _____

DAY 48 ───────────── DATE _____

A Word that Needs to Become Flesh: Koinōnia

"That you also may have fellowship with us; and indeed our fellowship is with the Father, and with His Son Jesus Christ" (1 John 1:3).

In the New Testament, the word *koinōnia* is most frequently used as a noun. When used as a noun, *koinōnia* means "fellowship" or "partnership." The word in contemporary Greek meant a business partnership, a marriage relationship, or a person's relationship with God. It is within the realm of this third meaning that the New Testament uses the word *koinōnia*.

Koinōnia was sometimes used in relationship to the sharing of friendship. Acts 2:42 says, "They were continually devoting themselves to the apostles' teaching and to fellowship." It was sometimes used in relation to the sharing of financial or material possession (Rom. 15:26 and Heb. 13:16). At least once *koinōnia* was used to refer to "participation in the gospel" (Phil. 1:5).

Koinōnia "of the Holy Spirit" is mentioned in 2 Corinthians 13:14 and in Philippians 2:1. *Koinōnia* with Christ is mentioned in 1 Corinthians 1:9, "God is faithful, through whom you were called into fellowship with His Son, Jesus Christ our Lord" as well as in 1 Corinthians 10:16 and Philippians 3:10. *Koinōnia* with God is referred to in 1 John 1:3, "Our fellowship is with the Father," and again in 1 John 1:6.

From the New Testament references, it seems we are to have fellowship or be in partnership with other human beings and with God (Father, Son, and Spirit).

How's your *koinōnia* with your fellow Christians? No, really, how is it? How about your *koinōnia* with God? This word needs to become flesh in us.

Reader's Response

A Prayer to Complete

God, I really want to have fellowship with You and with my fellow Christians. Show me today where I am lacking in these two relationships. May I become a "doer" of this word, not just a hearer only today as I . . .

Going Deeper

1. Acts 2:42-43 is a description of the life-style of some new believers. List the characteristics of this life-style as recorded in these verses.

    (1) _____
    (2) _____
    (3) _____
    (4) _____
    (5) _____
    (6) _____

2. What kind of fellowship resulted from the above type of life-style (Acts 2:44)?

3. What are three things you could do in your life to create the kind of results stated in Acts 2:44?

    (1) _____
    (2) _____
    (3) _____

4. What does it mean to you to have fellowship with Jesus Christ or with God?

5. How can you increase the quality of that fellowship this next week?

DAY 49 ————————— DATE _____

A Word that Needs to Become Flesh: *Koinōneō*

"Let the one who is taught share all good things with him who teaches" (Gal. 6:6).

A word that becomes flesh only in part causes an unbalanced life. *Koinōnia* is a noun and means "fellowship" or "partnership," but that is only part of its meaning. Used as a verb, it (*koinōneō*) means "to share." In contemporary Greek, *koinōneō* meant "to share in an action with another person" or "to share a common possession" or even "to share life."

In the New Testament, *Koinōneō* is used in four different ways. It is sometimes used to refer to sharing in humanity as in Hebrews 2:14. Frequently, *koinōneō* is used to refer to the sharing of things that are material as in Romans 12:13: "contributing to [or sharing in] the needs of the saints." This same type of sharing is found in Romans 15:27 and also in Galatians 6:6.

First Timothy 5:22 makes reference to a type of sharing that involves action. A final type of sharing is mentioned in 1 Peter 4:13 and deals with sharing in an experience, "but to the degree that you share the sufferings of Christ, keep on rejoicing; so that also at the revelation of His glory, you may rejoice with exultation."

Here, in a word, is the balance of the Christian witness. It is the balance of being and doing. We are in fellowship and partnership with others and with God. But we must also actively share that which we experience in fellowship with God and others. Sharing without the fellowship is self-powered sharing and will not endure. One without the other is an unbalanced witness. If you're going to be a word made flesh, be all of the word.

Reader's Response

A Prayer to Complete

Teach me today, Lord, how to be a balanced witness. Let me not be without doing nor let me do without being. May this word become flesh in my life today as I . . .

Going Deeper

1. How have you "shared" in material ways as recorded in Romans 12:13; Romans 15:27; or Galatians 6:6?
2. First Peter 4:13 discusses sharing in the suffering of Christ? How have you done this?
3. What does the above answer tell you about your life of "sharing" with Jesus?
4. React to the statement: "Sharing without the fellowship is self-powered sharing and will not endure."
5. List three ways you could actively translate the verb *koinōneō* into your life in the next week.
   (1) _____
   (2) _____
   (3) _____

DAY 50 ———————————————— DATE _____
A Word that Needs to Become Flesh: Power

"This is my work, and I can do it only because Christ's mighty energy is at work within me" (Col. 1:29, TLB).

The word in the New Testament that refers to the power of God is *energeia*. It is not used for God's potential. It is used for His actual power—power that was realized and felt. The word appears eight times in the New Testament and is sometimes translated "working."

In Ephesians 1:19-20 and in Colossians 2:12, the word is used to describe how God brought about the resurrection of Jesus. In Ephesians 4:16, *energeia* is used to describe how the body of Christ, the church, is held together. In Philippians 3:21, *energeia* describes how God will change human, earthly bodies into heavenly bodies at the second coming of Jesus Christ.

In Ephesians 3:7, Paul uses the same word to describe how he became a minister, and in Colossians 1:29, he refers to the power of God within him as that which enables him to labor or work.

Before you get too excited about potential power, you ought to know that twice *energeia* is used to refer to satanic power. In 2 Thessalonians 2:9 and again in 2:11, we read of Satan using *energeia*. This is proof that it is of value. If something works, Satan will attempt to prostitute it for his use. But the power belongs to God.

What would you be willing to give for that kind of power? Would it affect your labor and work if you had the kind of power that brings about resurrections and holds thousands of people together as one, and changes earthly life into heavenly life? Would you like to have it? Why not ask God for some *energeia?* Oh! Be careful how you use it!

Reader's Response

A Prayer to Complete

Lord, I believe You are all powerful. Help me to realize that the way to real power is through acknowledging my own weakness. I want to labor and work in Your power and not my own. Grant that I may be a good steward of Your power today as I . . .

Going Deeper

1. What is your reaction to the fact that the same *energeia* used to resurrect Jesus is available to you as a Christian?

2. In what three ways have you been a part of the *energeia* that holds the church together?
   (1) _____
   (2) _____
   (3) _____
3. In what ways has Colossians 1:29 been true in your experience during these hundred days of servanthood?
4. What are two ways that you have seen *energeia* misused these hundred days? Do you think these were of Satan?
   (1) _____
   (2) _____
5. What are three ways you could be a good steward or manager of God's power?
   (1) _____
   (2) _____
   (3) _____

DAY 51 ———————————— DATE _____
A Special Word For God

"Abba! Father!" (Mark 14:36; Rom. 8:15; Gal. 4:6).

When children want something really special, they have an extra special way of saying "Daddy." I know when I hear "Daddy" in that special tone of voice that a special request will follow. In a similar way the children of Jesus' day said "Abba" to their earthly fathers. It was a special word for the father.

Three times in the New Testament "Abba" is used, and the three tell us something of our new relationship with God our Heavenly Father. In Mark 14:36, Jesus Himself, in the midst of the Gethsemane agony, cried, "Abba! Father!" as He struggled with His soon-coming crucifixion. On our behalf, He employed a special word for God.

In Romans 8:15 we are told that we have received a "spirit of adoption as sons by which we cry out, 'Abba! Father!' " At conversion, when God becomes our own personal Heavenly Father, we are allowed to use this special word to address Him. We can now use it because we have become "heirs of God, and fellow-heirs with Christ" (Rom. 8:17).

In Galatians 4:6, a final privilege is awarded us in relation to this name of Abba. "Because you are sons, God has sent forth the Spirit of His Son into our hearts, crying 'Abba! Father!'" Now it is Jesus Himself, in us by way of the Holy Spirit, Who speaks with us and intercedes for us before the Father with this special word, "Abba! Father!"

Reader's Response

A Prayer to Complete

Thank You, God, for allowing me to call You "Abba! Father!" Thank You for allowing me through Your indwelling Spirit to have this special access to You. May I use it wisely today as I . . .

Going Deeper

1. What special word do (or did) you use for your earthly father? What meaning did this word have to you?
2. What word do you use for God when you are making requests of Him? What meaning does it have?
3. What does it mean to you when the writer says of Jesus, "On our behalf, He employed a special word for God"?
4. Since God is special, what four things would you like to tell Him today?

    (1) _____

    (2) _____

    (3) _____

    (4) _____

DAY 52 ———————————— DATE _____
Drinking from Dry Brooks

"It happened after a while, that the brook dried up" (1 Kings 17:7).

The land went dry. But in the midst of the drought, God provided sustenance for His servant Elijah. God instructed Elijah to "hide . . . by the brook Cherith," and there he would "drink of the brook" (1 Kings 17:3-4).

When drought is taking place, God provides sustenance for His servants. Perhaps in your situation, as you seek to minister in a sometimes "dry land," you have discovered a "brook Cherith." God has provided a way whereby you can gain strength for your ministry. Maybe your brook is a person whom you've come to appreciate. Or maybe it is a church fellowship that nourishes you regularly. Or maybe it is the hope of some fulfilled dream or plan. Be careful! The same God Who provides a brook for nourishment allows the brook to run dry for dependence.

No doubt Elijah protested, at least to himself, when the brook dried up. How can one drink from a dry brook? God had led him there and provided it for him, but now it was dry. Elijah needed to learn, and we do too, that sustenance comes from God and God alone.

Sometimes the best of friends fail us. Sometimes the warmest of church fellowships falter. Sometimes the brightest hopes have a way of being destroyed or deferred. But God is always present—present to lead us on to other brooks—other sources of sustenance.

Be sure your faith is based on God, not in God's brooks. The best of brooks dry up, but God never fails. He always leads us on to other brooks. You are a pilgrim traveler, not a brook worshiper. You can't drink from a dry brook.

Reader's Response

A Prayer to Complete

Lead me, Father, to place my faith in You for provision and sustenance. May I drink today from You and having been nourished may I become Your brook to . . .

Going Deeper

1. What evidences (or potentials) are there of drought in your situation.
   (1) _____
   (2) _____
   (3) _____
2. What has been your "brook Cherith"?
3. Can you react to the statement: "The same God Who provides a brook for nourishment allows the brook to run dry for dependence"?
4. In what two ways are you depending on God today?
   (1) _____
   (2) _____
5. React to the statement: "You are a pilgrim traveler, not a brook worshiper."

DAY 53 ━━━━━━━━━━━━━━ DATE _____
Tension

"The good that I wish, I do not do" (Rom. 7:19).

Have you had one of those nights lately where sleep had to wait until your mind replayed the events of the day over and over? You lay there on the bed so tension filled that you could not sleep? Let's identify a possible reason and locate a solution.

There was just so much to do that particular day. There were so many people you had to serve, so many relationships you had to live within. There was a lot expected of you on that day. Sound familiar?

Whatever standard of achievement was set for you or which you set for yourself, it was no doubt less demanding than the goal Jesus expressed for His disciples in the Sermon on the Mount when He said, "You are to be perfect, as your heavenly Father is perfect" (Matt. 5:48).

Thus we have the standard or goal for the day—either perfection as Jesus expressed it or something less as we apply it to our situation. Then there is the status quo of much of the world around us. In between the goal and the status quo is the tension. Paul discovered tension and expressed his feelings in these words, "For the good that I wish, I do not do; but I practice the very evil that I do not wish" (Rom. 7:19).

You are being pulled from two directions. On the one hand, your own goal and God's standard of perfection pull you upward and onward. On the other hand, the world around you, the status quo, and your own sinful nature pull you downward and backward. You are caught in the tension.

Do two things. Thank God for the tension; for without it your goals would sink to the level of the status quo. Second, make a habit of "casting all your anxiety upon Him, because He cares for you" (1 Pet. 5:7).

Reader's Response

A Prayer to Complete

Lord, thank You for the tension that makes life an exciting adventure. Help me today to spend more time involved in the tension than I spend time worrying about it. May I see the value of my tension in . . .

Going Deeper
1. Read Romans 7:1-25. Try to describe in one sentence the tension that Paul was experiencing as he wrote these words.
2. State in one sentence your personal goal for these hundred days of servanthood.
3. On the instrument below mark where you think you are in the process of achieving your goal with *0* being where you started and *10* being the achieving of your goal.

---

   0   1   2   3   4   5   6   7   8   9   10

4. Identify some of the tension which you have been feeling or now feel.
5. In addition to "casting all your anxiety upon Him," list some other things you can do to relate to your tension and move toward your goal?

   (1) _____
   (2) _____
   (3) _____
   (4) _____

DAY 54 ——————————— DATE _____
Doing God's Will

"I delight to do Thy will, O my God" (Ps. 40:8).

Many Christians spend a lot of time struggling with the decision of whether or not to do what they know to be God's will. Some suffer long sleepless nights and strained relationships before arriving at any understanding of the rightness of the decision. Then they experience the joy of having found God's will and the fulfillment of doing it.

This psalm tells us of one who has suffered, then found relief, and now responds in praise and obedience to God. His expression of delight is found in doing God's will.

The will of God will be done, whether we do it or not. He

is not dependent on us for the accomplishment of His will. Had you not answered His call for your particular area of service, He would have found someone else or some other way of accomplishing His will. The delight comes when we realize that even though He doesn't need us, He wants us. What a privilege!

We should do God's will whether we delight in it or not. Sometimes we do His will with reluctance. Even Jesus, about whom this psalm may be speaking, seemed to be a bit reluctant as He struggled with God's will in the garden of Gethsemane. The discipline of doing God's will, though every fiber of our being is reluctant, will result in a new freedom with which to live. And that will in turn bring delight to our life.

Doing God's will will draw you ever near to Jesus even to the closeness of family. "Whoever shall do the will of My Father who is in heaven, he is My brother and sister and mother" (Matt. 12:50). And that brings delight in knowing you are that close to Jesus.

Do His will today, and delight in it.

Reader's Response

A Prayer to Complete

Lord, I will do Your will today as best I understand it. May I do it not out of fear but with delight. I will especially do Your will related to . . .

Going Deeper

1. Recall three reasons why you almost did not follow God's will in a recent situation.

    (1) _____

    (2) _____

    (3) _____

2. How do these reasons look to you now?

3. Why do you think God wanted you to follow His will in that situation?
4. List three ways that you "delight" to do God's will.
   (1) _____
   (2) _____
   (3) _____
5. How do you feel about the statement, "The discipline of doing God's will, though every fiber of our being is reluctant, will result in a new freedom with which to live"?

DAY 55 ———————————— DATE _____
God's Why to Your Where Is Sometimes a When

"For such a time as this" (Esther 4:14). "The fulness of the times" (Eph. 1:10).

No doubt by this time in your hundred days you have begun to wonder just why you are in your particular place of service. There could be, and no doubt are, many logical reasons. Otherwise you would probably have been elsewhere. Perhaps your special talents or gifts were needed to meet a job description. Or maybe it was felt that your personality was an exact fit to your situation. Still again you may have blended in well with a team of workers. The logical reasons will need to be discovered by you.

Esther wondered why she had been placed by God in her particular situation. She was surrounded by death plots and deception, and she searched for why she was there. Mordecai, having already shared with her some logical reasons in terms of her best interests, shared with her that she was present due to a higher reason. "Who knows whether you have not attained royalty for such a time as this?" (Esther 4:14). In addition to logical callings, Esther had a higher calling from God, and she was present in a "fulness of the times."

The longer the life, the stronger the belief that everything that happens in God's will happens in the fullness of time. You may not yet fully understand why you are where you are, but be assured of this: if you went there under the leadership of God, you are there at the right time. You have been placed in your place "for such a time as this." God makes no mistakes. Perhaps today, God, who knows you better than you know yourself, will reveal to you His "fulness of the times" for your situation. God's why to your where is sometimes a when.

Reader's Response

A Prayer to Complete

Lord, help me to understand how You conceive of time and space. Lead me to the knowledge that *when* has a lot to do with *where,* and sometimes both explain the *why* of Your will. May I do Your will here and now as I . . .

Going Deeper

1. What are two logical reasons why God placed you in your particular situation?
    (1) _____
    (2) _____
2. What evidences are there that you are serving in your situation in a "fulness of the times"?
    (1) _____
    (2) _____
    (3) _____
    (4) _____
3. What do you think is meant by the title "God's Why to Your Where Is Sometimes a When"?
4. Esther's reply to Mordecai (Esther 4:16) was, "If I perish, I perish." How does her reply to the "fulness of the times" apply to your life?
5. Do you agree or disagree that "everything that happens in God's will happens in the fullness of time"?

DAY 56 ———————————— DATE _____
A Word that Does Not Need to Become Flesh: Defeat

"For the Lord had ordained to defeat the good counsel of Ahithophel" (2 Sam. 17:14, RSV).

In 2 Samuel 17 the basic decision facing Absalom was how to battle David. Ahithophel favored an immediate attack on David. This was the logical move, and for many reasons made more sense than any of the other alternatives. Hushai on the other hand recommended an alternate plan which was such a departure from sound wisdom and logic that it brought about a rare editorial comment from the author. The plan of Hushai was understandable only if "the Lord had ordained to defeat the good counsel of Ahithophel" (2 Sam. 17:14, RSV).

Has the idea of defeat crept into your ministry lately? Did you realize that the word *defeat* is mentioned only twice in the Bible and both times in the Old Testament? (2 Sam. 15:34 and 2 Sam. 17:14). Not only is it not mentioned in the New Testament but most modern translations of the Bible leave the word *defeat* out altogether. You might say that the word *defeat* is not in God's vocabulary for the believer.

It looked like sure defeat for Paul in jail at Philippi until he led the jailer to Christ. Again it seemed defeat was imminent as Paul stood before the judge and the judge replied, "Paul, 'In a short time you will persuade me to become a Christian'" (Acts 26:28). But even in chains, Paul turned defeat into victory by writing letters.

The danger involved is not from defeat but from the fear of defeat. God will not allow you to be defeated. Nor is the fear born of God. "God hath not given us the spirit of fear; but of power, and of love, and of a sound mind" (2 Tim. 1:7, KJV). Stop fearing defeat. Start experiencing victory. It's God's way.

Reader's Response

A Prayer to Complete

God, forgive me for being overly concerned with defeat.
May I face today, assured of the victory that is found in You.
Thank You for the following evidences of victory . . .

Going Deeper

1. Are there some things about your situation that make sense
    only because God is in them? What are these?
2. What are some things that could cause you to feel defeated?
    (1) _____
    (2) _____
    (3) _____
    (4) _____
3. In what ways has God helped you to overcome the above
    items?
    (1) _____
    (2) _____
    (3) _____
    (4) _____
4. Name one way God has given you a spirit of each of the
    following this week (2 Tim. 1:7):
    (1) Power: _____
    (2) Love: _____
    (3) Sound mind (discipline): _____
5. What is one evidence of victory which you sense today?

DAY 57 ──────────── DATE _____

A Word that Does Not Need to Become Flesh: Despair

"We are troubled on every side, yet not distressed; we are perplexed, but not in despair" (2 Cor. 4:8 KJV).

"Today I hit the depths of despair," said the Christian servant to her minister. Do you know the feeling? Let's take a look at the subject.

From the biblical perspective the word *despair* is mentioned only four times (1 Sam. 27:1; Eccl. 2:20; 2 Cor. 1:8; 4:8). Despair comes from a lack of recognition of one's dependence upon others. We sometimes try to do the job all alone. Despair also comes from conviction of our own sin or sometimes conviction that the demands on us are too great. Occasionally, despair comes from a lack of trust in God. More often than not it is from a combination of these causes.

Despair becomes sin as it leads us to question the mercy, the goodness, and the faithfulness of God. The Bible tells us that all things work for our good if we love God and are called according to His purpose (Rom. 8:28). Despair is not discouragement. We all have discouragement from time to time. Despair is not anxiety. This usually comes from an excess of fear.

Despair is losing all hope. It is the abandonment of the pilgrimage toward the final goal. We deal with despair by realizing that as creatures in God's image we were created not for despair but for hope. Joel discovered this and wrote, "The Lord will be the hope of his people" (Joel 3:16, KJV), and Paul penned the answer in these words, "Christ in you, the hope of glory" (Col. 1:27). Hope is despair remade in God's image.

Reader's Response

A Prayer to Complete

Father, when despair seeks to invade my life, fill me with hope. As I minister today, guide me to see my circumstances through eyes of hope, not despair. One evidence of hope may be seen today in . . .

112

Going Deeper

1. What conditions or circumstances could potentially lead you to despair?

   (1) _____

   (2) _____

2. List three reasons you are thankful for Christian friends.

   (1) _____

   (2) _____

   (3) _____

3. In what ways have you felt God's help and support during your hundred days of servanthood?

4. Is there some sin in your life that would cause you to despair?

5. Having listed reasons you are thankful for human support, acknowledging God's support and confronting your own sin, how do the conditions listed in question one look now?

6. React to the statement: "Hope is despair remade in God's image."

DAY 58 ———————————— DATE _____

A Word that Does Not Need to Become Flesh: Quarrel

"Do not quarrel on the journey" (Gen. 45:24).

The story of Joseph and his brothers is a familiar one. Because Joseph was his father's favorite, his brothers in an act of jealousy sold him as a slave to a band of Midianites on their way to Egypt. As time went by, Canaan suffered a drought, and Jacob sent his sons to Egypt to buy food. There they found Joseph in a place of responsibility. After a second visit Joseph sent them home to bring their father back to Egypt, and, "as they departed, he said to them, 'Do not quarrel on the journey.'"

Have you found yourself quarreling along the journey? Has it reached a point with a friend or family member of an associate where tension is the mood of the day? Regardless of your feelings you should not "quarrel on the journey" for the same reasons that applied to the brothers of Joseph.

One reason for their not quarreling was that they were brothers. Their family ties were too strong to be threatened by quarreling. Dissension among Christian friends becomes even more shameful because we are not a physical family but a spiritual family. We eat at the same spiritual table and work in the same vineyard and rest in the same Lord.

They should not quarrel because of the message which they carried. They were to tell Jacob his favorite son was alive. It was to be the best news Jacob recently heard. So is your message to a hurting world. The Son is not dead; He is alive and bids you come to Him. Their quarreling would hinder the telling of their message. And the same is true for you. The "journey" is too crucial to take time out for quarreling among the travelers.

Reader's Response

A Prayer to Complete

Father, forgive me for quarreling or even for thoughts in that direction. Help me today to get on with the purpose of the "journey" which I understand to include . . .

Going Deeper

1. What are some reasons that Joseph warned his brothers not to "quarrel on the journey"? What made him suspect that they might quarrel?
   (1) _____
   (2) _____
   (3) _____
2. What are some reasons that you have been tempted to "quarrel on the journey"?
   (1) _____

    (2) _____

    (3) _____

    (4) _____

3. Examine each of the above reasons. Why would each be a detriment to your ministry?

    (1) _____

    (2) _____

    (3) _____

    (4) _____

4. Is there someone with whom you've quarreled during these hundred days? Perhaps you need to talk with that person and correct any negative feelings.

5. React to the statement: "The 'journey' is too crucial to take time out for quarreling among the travelers."

DAY 59 ━━━━━━━━━━━━━ DATE _____

Get Away and Pray

"He arose and went out" (Mark 1:35). "He departed to the mountain to pray" (Mark 6:46). "He went a little beyond them" (Mark 14:35).

Our Lord needed to get away on occasion and pray to His Father. Early in His ministry, following an outpouring of compassion in the synagogue to a man possessed by an unclean spirit, Jesus felt the need of being alone in prayer, and "in the early morning, while it was still dark, He arose and went out and departed to a lonely place, and was praying there" (Mark 1:35).

Again, in the midst of His public ministry, Jesus took His disciples across the Sea of Galilee only to find a crowd of hungry people. After the teaching and feeding of the multitude, Jesus sent the disciples to the boat, dismissed the crowd, and "He departed to the mountain to pray" (Mark 6:46).

Late in the public ministry of Jesus, He left His disciples

behind, "And He went a little beyond them, and fell to the ground, and began praying" (Mark 14:35).

In all three cases, Jesus left a crowd to be alone in prayer. He deliberately made Himself unavailable to them. His action was not out of unconcern or the lack of love. In fact, it was because of concern and love that He departed often. Our love and concern for people is not effective enough if we are always with them. We must depart occasionally. Service is more effective if it is broken occasionally by departures for prayer. The responsibility to be alone for prayer is as much a religious responsibility as is the responsibility to serve. You need to get away and pray.

But Jesus never stayed away long at a time. Once He was interrupted by the disciples and told, "Everyone is looking for You" (Mark 1:37). Once He hurried back to His responsibilities. Once He was interrupted by a multitude led by Judas.

In the midst of service you will not have long to pray, but pray you must. Find time today to get away and pray.

Reader's Response

A Prayer to Complete

Lord, I have been too much caught up in service to attend to the inner source of support. Help me to find time today to get away and pray with You because I especially need to talk with You about . . .

Going Deeper

1. In the three Scripture passages, see if you can determine a reason why Jesus left the group for privacy and prayer.
   (1) Mark 1:32-39 _____
   (2) Mark 6:30-56 _____
   (3) Mark 14:32-46 _____
2. From these passages what appears to be the immediate result of Jesus' prayer time?

116

    (1) Mark 1:32-39 _____

    (2) Mark 6:30-56 _____

    (3) Mark 14:32-46 _____

3. Have you had a recent need to get away and pray? Whether you succeeded in getting away or not, what was the result of your experience?

4. Respond to the statement: "The responsibility to be alone for prayer is as much a religious responsibility as is the responsibility to serve."

5. What is one way you could balance your service today or tomorrow with your need for privacy and prayer?

DAY 60 ——————————— DATE _____

Plural Ability

"We are able" (Mark 10:39).

Following a series of very meaningful and impressive encounters in the life of Jesus, two of His disciples came to Him with a request. James and John asked of Him if they could "sit in Your glory, one on Your right, and one on Your left"(v. 37).

Their bold request was met with Jesus' answer, "You do not know what you are asking for" (v. 38). After explaining to them that such a request also involved drinking of "The cup that I drink" and being baptized with "the baptism with which I am baptized," Jesus asked them, "Are you able?" (v. 38).

Their answer was more profound than even they realized. "We are able" (v. 39) implies a plural ability. Neither was able, nor could have ever been able, alone. Only as a part of the family of God with Jesus could they ever possibly be able.

Are you able to serve Jesus Christ? Are you able to do the countless tasks assigned to you? Are you able to work sometimes long, hard hours? Are you able to minister without visible proof or results? Are you able to pay the price—to drink the "cup" or participate in the "baptism"?

Your answer must not be, "I am able," for you are not, nor can you ever be. Your answer must be, "We are able," for only as a part of a team and only alongside of Jesus can you ever hope to be able. You will never be able, but God working with and through you is able.

Jesus later was indignant with James and John and assured them such ambition for greatness must begin with servanthood. "Whoever wishes to be first among you shall be slave of all" (Mark 10:44). Plural ability begins with singular servanthood.

Reader's Response

A Prayer to Complete

Lord, make me aware of opportunities of service today, and may I lean on the strength of others and You as I serve. I am thankful for fellow servants such as . . .

Going Deeper

1. Read Mark 10:35-45. Why was the request of James and John so bold?
2. How do you evaluate the question of James and John in light of what Jesus had already told His disciples in Matthew 7:7-8 and would later tell them in John 14:13-14?
3. What is your reaction to the bold answer to Jesus' question: "We are able" (Mark 10:39)? How do you think Jesus reacted?
4. The idea of "plural ability" suggests that you need the support system of co-workers. Name three persons who help make up your support system.
   (1) _____
   (2) _____
   (3) _____
   _____
5. What is your reaction to the statement: "Plural ability be-

gins with singular servanthood"? What are some ways you
have discovered this to be true?

DAY 61 ———————————— DATE ——————————
Temptation

"Tempted in all things" (Heb. 4:15).

It's all right to be tempted. Jesus with purpose allowed Himself to be tempted by Satan. It happened numerous times in His
ministry, but never as clearly nor as applicable to you as when
Jesus was tempted in the early days of His ministry as recorded
in Matthew 4:1-11.

Jesus was tempted in three areas. First, Satan confronted
Him in the physical area. After forty days of fasting Jesus was
obviously hungry, and Satan knew it. The temptation to "command that these stones become bread" (Matt. 4:3) was aimed
not at a weak point in Jesus' life but at a strong point. Sure
Jesus was hungry, but, if He had abstained from food for forty
days, could He not endure one more day? Satan often hits at
your strong point, reasoning if you yield there you will yield
anywhere.

Second, Satan tempted Jesus in the spiritual area. The request to "throw Yourself down" (Matt. 4:6) was aimed at the
level of trust which Jesus had in His Father. Satan wanted Jesus
to put God to the test. Had Jesus jumped, it would not have
proven trust but the lack of it. If we really trust, it is not
necessary to test. It is when our trust wavers that we test.

Third, Satan tempted Jesus in the material area. The offer
that "All these things I will give You, if You fall down and
worship me" (Matt. 4:9) was particularly tempting since it was
these "kingdoms" that Jesus came to claim as His own possession. These were to become "the kingdom of our Lord, and of
His Christ" (Rev. 11:15). Satan often offers shortcuts. Usually,
they are things that are not his to give in the first place.

Jesus was "tempted in all things as we are" (Heb. 4:15). No area of your life will face temptation that was not first faced by Jesus. It's OK to be tempted, *BUT*, Jesus did not yield to His temptations. Yielding is sin. Satan only tempts those who are a threat to him. Rejoice in your temptations, *BUT*, do not yield to them.

Reader's Response

A Prayer to Complete

Father, thank You for allowing Your Son to experience temptation in "all things." Help me today to follow His example of resisting temptation especially that temptation that I know I'll face today related to . . .

Going Deeper

1. List a recent temptation in each of the following areas:
   (1) Physical_____
   (2) Spiritual_____
   (3) Material_____
2. How can the example of Jesus in Matthew 4:1-11 strengthen you in each of the above temptations?
   (1) _____
   (2) _____
   (3) _____
3. How has Satan tempted you at your strong point during these hundred days of servanthood?
4. Has Satan offered any "shortcuts" to you in these hundred days? How have you resisted or yielded to these?
5. React to the statement: "Satan only tempts those who are a threat to him."

DAY 62 ────────────────── DATE _____

Dealing with Temptation

"Tempted in all things . . . yet without sin" (Heb. 4:15).

"I must be doing a good job 'cause Satan has sure been on me lately." The young man was right. He was doing a good "job," and that was exactly why Satan was "on" him. So how do you deal with temptation. Here are several suggestions.

Don't blame your temptations on God. He did not promise you a ministry apart from temptation, but He did promise to stand with you. Read 1 Corinthians 10:13 and James 1:13-15.

If you know that you cannot deal with a particular temptation, ask God to help you avoid it and work at getting strong enough in your Christian life to live with the temptation. Jesus taught the disciples to pray, "Do not lead us into temptation" (Matt. 6:13).

When Jesus was tempted (Matt. 4:1-11), in each instance He responded to Satan by quoting Scripture. If you are going to serve God, you had better build up your arsenal of ammunition for your battle with Satan. Scripture memory is an excellent weapon when used properly.

Rejoice when you are tempted. James told us to "count it all joy when ye fall into divers temptations; knowing this, that the trying of your faith worketh patience" (Jas. 1:2-3, KJV).

When you have successfully resisted temptation, get ready to be ministered unto. After Jesus' encounter with Satan we are told that "the devil left Him; and behold, angels came and began to minister to Him" (Matt. 4:11). It's worth the battle to experience the victory.

Reader's Response

A Prayer to Complete

Thank you, God, for the temptations that will come my way today. Give me strength to deal with them in a manner that would be pleasing to You. I pray that You would lead me from temptation related to . . .

Going Deeper

1. What have you blamed on God lately? Does 1 Corinthians 10:13 and James 1:13-15 speak to this blame?
2. Think of a recent temptation in your life. Who led you into temptation?
3. What are three Scripture verses that you could memorize this week that would help you resist temptation?
   (1) _____
   (2) _____
   (3) _____
4. After the temptation experience of Jesus, the "angels came and began to minister to Him" (Matt. 4:11). What application does this have to you?
5. Do you agree or disagree with the statement, "It's worth the battle to experience the victory"?

DAY 63 ——————————— DATE _____
Without Water

"Springs [or wells] without water, and mists driven by a storm" (2 Pet. 2:17). "Clouds without water, carried along by winds" (Jude 12).

Peter described false teachers as "springs [or wells] without water." In Palestine, a spring (or well) of water was one of the best of earthly things. The saddest of sights was a thirsty pilgrim arriving in vain at a dry spring (or well).

Most have experienced the reality of the illustration used in Jude 12, especially at a time of year when the land becomes parched and begins to crack from the lack of rain. Temperatures soar, and we hope and sometimes pray for the cooling, refreshing rain. Occasional low-hanging clouds roll in and promise relief. Then, with hopes high, the wind carries them away without a drop of rain.

Jude understood the situation of his day and likened it to

this illustration. "Certain persons" had "crept in unnoticed" (Jude 4) and had held out for the people false hope. In begging the believers to "contend earnestly for the faith" (Jude 3), Jude refers to these false teachers as "clouds without water, carried along by winds" (Jude 12).

Wherever you serve, there are those needy persons who made your field of service like that of David who wrote of his: "My soul thirsts for Thee, my flesh yearns for Thee, In a dry and weary land where there is no water. (Ps. 63:1). Your presence offers a ray of hope. You are like low-hanging clouds. The question, then, is: Will you be able to present unto them that which will satisfy their spiritual drought, or will you too be a cloud or spring "without water" driven by the "wind" or "storm"?

If the answer is no, perhaps a quick trip back to the well is in order. If the answer is yes, get on with passing the cup of water in His name.

Reader's Response

A Prayer to Complete

Lord, make me an instrument of refreshment to thirsty souls today. May I drink quickly, then offer a cup of water in Your name to . . .

Going Deeper

1. Has anyone ever offered you what proved to be false hope? How did you feel?
2. What are three ways you could "contend earnestly for the faith" (Jude 3) during these hundred days of servanthood?
   (1) _____
   (2) _____
   (3) _____
3. Are there two persons in your field of service who make

your field of service like that described by David in Psalm
63:1? Who are these people?

(1) _____

(2) _____

4. In what ways can you offer these two persons a real thirst
   quencher rather than just "clouds without water"?
5. What could you do today to either make a "quick trip back
   to the well" or "get on with passing the cup of water in His
   name"?

DAY 64 ——————————————— DATE _____

Remade

"But the vessel that he was making of clay was spoiled in
the hand of the potter; so he remade it into another vessel, as
it pleased the potter to make" (Jer. 18:4).

What happened? Several months ago you had it all together
in your mind. Christian servant! You were called and ready.
But nobody told you all these little details did they? Somehow
as the days went on your idea of ministry cracked and shat-
tered into pieces. Disappointment set in followed by questions.

Jeremiah could identify with you. Having done all he knew
to do, the people were still headed for destruction. His heart
was breaking. Then God led him to the workbench of the
potter. Jeremiah watched as the potter molded and shaped a
piece of clay into an object of beauty. But just before completion, the object turned out to be "imperfect" (GNB). Rather
than take a new piece of clay the potter reused the clay on the
wheel and "remade it into another vessel."

There come those times and places in our lives when we
become imperfect in the Potter's hands. God uses these occasions to "remake" us into that which pleases Him.

Perhaps your days are not all you expected them to be. Or
perhaps you have turned out to be less than you were expected

to be. Maybe something has happened that has caused a crack in the vessel. Will God have to look for more clay, wait for another servant, or will you allow the sometimes painful "remaking" process to begin in your life?

Reader's Response

A Prayer to Complete

God, if I need to be broken further help me to endure the pain. Give me the courage to allow You the freedom to remake me in a way that pleases You today. I need to be remade in

. . .

Going Deeper

1. What are two expectations you had for your hundred days that have not yet been seen?

    (1) _____

    (2) _____

2. Do these expectations need to be reevaluated? Are they still realistic? Do you have new expectations or need to develop some?

3. Have you ever had an experience like that described by Jeremiah? Have you ever felt that God took the pieces of your life and "remade" you? Describe your feelings.

4. Is there a possibility that you are not all God intended you to be at this point in your life? Do you need to be remade in any area of your ministry?

5. There are no doubt persons around you who's lives are broken. How could you serve as a "Potter's Helper" and help in the remaking process?

DAY 65 ─────────────── DATE ──────────────
When to Let Them Go

"He went away grieved" (Mark 10:22).

What a prospect! He was rich (Luke 18:23). That certainly would have been a boost to the struggling groups of believers as they tried to reach out with the good news. He was young (Matt. 19:20). Youth with its enthusiasm and drive, is to be desired. He was a man of position—a ruler (Luke 18:18). A prominent citizen could certainly have given the new group status and respectability. What a prospect!

After Jesus had shared with this rich young ruler the answer to his question: "What shall I do to inherit eternal life?" (Mark 10:17), the young man "went away grieved." The demands of Jesus were too tough. The way presented was too difficult. The cost was too high. He wanted eternal life, but not enough to pay the price.

No doubt in your ministry of these hundred days you have encountered someone like this man, and you have wished so much that he would believe. You have shared the good news with him, and he wants so much to accept it but cannot quite pay the price. Perhaps he is just not willing to give up some things that are now a part of his life. Or he cannot quite accept some Christian principle.

What are you going to do? His conversion would mean so very much to the group, not to mention to him personally. Are you going to lower the standards to get him in? Will you water down the gospel to make it acceptable to him? Will you stretch the truth until he likes it? No! You will follow the example of Jesus.

Surely Jesus did some other things. Perhaps He tried to make later contact with the young man or spent much time in prayer for him and no doubt grieved Himself. The one thing we know for sure is what Jesus did not do. He did not lower the standard. He let the young man go. Be firm in your convictions both as you live them and as you share them.

Reader's Response

A Prayer to Complete

Dear Lord, forgive me for compromise or for even the thoughts of compromising my convictions. Help me to share the gospel as it is and trust You with the results. Especially help me today as I . . .

Going Deeper

1. Is there someone you wish would become a part of the fellowship of Christians where you serve? List some desireable characteristics of this person.

   (1) _____

   (2) _____

   (3) _____

   (4) _____

2. In what ways have you or someone you know shared the gospel with this person?

3. What could this person mean to the Christian group? What could the group mean to this person?

4. In Mark 10:24 Jesus indicated that it was difficult to enter the kingdom of God. Why is it difficult?

5. List a three-point strategy that could be employed on the person described above.

   (1) _____

   (2) _____

   (3) _____

DAY 66 ————————————— DATE _____

Strength in Weakness

"Conflicts without, fears within" (2 Cor. 7:5).

While writing to the Christians in Corinth, Paul remembered an earlier experience. He had arrived in Macedonia a victim of physical strain and exhaustion. Unlike some of the "superapostles" around Corinth, Paul was very much aware and willing to acknowledge his physical limitations. He said, "We were afflicted on every side." He suffered from outer conflict—opposition from the opponents of the gospel he proclaimed. He suffered from inner fear—anxiety over how things were in Corinth. Paul was tired.

Sound familiar? Have your days gotten too long for your nights? Has the work of the ministry become more work than ministry? Have inner frustrations and outward conflicts taken their toll on your body, spirit, and mind? Cheer up! Look at Paul.

Paul's situation changed with the coming of Titus. Paul said, "God, who comforts the depressed, comforted us by the coming of Titus" (v. 6).

You will have conflicts, both from without and from within but draw strength from God's Word. "Be strong and courageous, do not be afraid or tremble at them, for the Lord your God is the one who goes with you, He will not fail you or forsake you" (Deut. 31:6).

And again, "Be strong and courageous, and act; do not fear nor be dismayed, for the Lord God, my God, is with you. He will not fail you nor forsake you until all the work for the service of the house of the Lord is finished" (1 Chron. 28:20).

In God's promises and plans there is enough strength to see you through.

Reader's Response

A Prayer to Complete

Lord, be my strength when I get tired and restore me to my

proper place of service in your time. Today I need your presence related to . . .

Going Deeper

1. Have you identified your limitations? What outside conflicts have you endured?
   - (1) _____
   - (2) _____
   - (3) _____
   - (4) _____
2. What inner fears or anxieties have you endured recently?
   - (1) _____
   - (2) _____
   - (3) _____
   - (4) _____
3. Name one person who has been a source of encouragement to you as Titus was for Paul.
4. List some of the resources you have had in these hundred days that have helped you cope with your outward conflicts and inward fears.
   - (1) _____
   - (2) _____
   - (3) _____
5. As you approach the next few weeks of your hundred days of servanthood, identify some areas of your life where you need the strength that God has promised to give you.
   - (1) _____
   - (2) _____
   - (3) _____
6. What would you need to do to obtain this strength?

DAY 67 ————————————— DATE ————————————

When Sacrifice Fails to Impress

"I desire . . . not sacrifice" (Matt. 9:13).

To be a Christian servant you really made a sacrifice. Just think (if you haven't already done so) how much money you could have made at another job, or by neglecting this role of servant. Think of the sacrifice of time with family and friends. You really are to be commended for that which you have given up—commended by men. God is not impressed.

Hosea said that God was not delighted. "For I delight in loyalty rather than sacrifice/And in the knowledge of God rather than burnt offerings" (Hos. 6:6). According to Hosea, God is more impressed with how you relate to Him than what you give up for Him.

Micah asked, "With what shall I come to the Lord/And bow myself before the God on high?" (Mic. 6:6). Then he listed several possibilities all in the area of sacrifice. His final conclusion was that the Lord did not require sacrifice, but He desired His followers to "do justice, to love kindness,/And to walk humbly" (v. 8). According to Micah, God is more impressed with how you live for Him than what you sacrifice for Him.

After an encounter with the Pharisees in which they challenged Him, Jesus told them to "go and learn what this means, 'I desire compassion, and not sacrifice' " (Matt. 9:13). According to Jesus, God is more impressed by our compassion than He is by our sacrifice.

You may have made great sacrifices and given up much to serve God during these hundred days. You are commended. But God will be more impressed with how you live for and relate to Him day by day.

Reader's Response

A Prayer to Complete

Father, forgive me for glorifying my sacrifices and help me

today to walk worthy of your calling especially as I walk
. . .

Going Deeper

1. What are three things you gave up to be a Christian servant especially for these hundred days?

   (1) _____

   (2) _____

   (3) _____

2. What are three things you have gained by being a Christian servant especially during these hundred days?

   (1) _____

   (2) _____

   (3) _____

3. Which is more impressive to you—that which you gave up or that which you gained? Which is more impressive to God?

4. What do you think Jesus meant when He said, "I desire compassion, and not sacrifice" (Matt. 9:13)? How does this apply to you?

5. What are two things in your hundred days of service with which you think God is pleased?

   (1) _____

   (2) _____

DAY 68 ——————————— DATE _____

Rain! Rain! Go Away!

"He leads me beside . . . waters" (Ps. 23:2).

Our house had already been flooded once, and several times during the past year the water had risen significantly in our yard. Part of living on a Georgia creek is experiencing the rapid and, sometimes, destructive rise of that creek during heavy rains. We had experienced it once, and that made me a bit anxious every time a hard rain began to fall.

That's why I was so uneasy in the worship service. Even though all was well on the inside of the worship center this particular Sunday, on the outside I could hear loud, heavy rain falling, and I observed some of my fellow worshipers entering the building with rain-soaked clothing. Nor did it help me relax when one person sat near me and said, to no one in specific, "It's like a hurricane out there." Having spent several years on the Texas gulf coast, those words only added to my worry. I wanted very much for the rain to go away.

Approximately twenty minutes into the service, we were invited to stand and sing, "He Leadeth Me!" The second verse had never spoken to me as clearly as it did on this day. With rain falling on the outside, we sang, "Sometimes 'mid scenes of deepest gloom,/Sometimes where Eden's bowers bloom,/By waters still, o'er troubled sea,/Still 'tis His hand that leadeth me!"

It is true that some rain will fall on each person but, before you wish yours away, allow God to lead you through some of it.

Reader's Response

A Prayer to Complete
Lord of sunshine and rain, I thank You for both and ask that on this day, You will lead me in the rain of . . .

Going Deeper
1. Can you identify some of the "rain" that has fallen in your life recently? What was your reaction to the experience?
2. How did Jesus lead you through the above experience, or if He did not, why do you think He did not?

3. It is easy to experience difficulties in the "rough water" times. Have you ever had difficulty when everything appeared to be going smoothly?

4. How can Jesus Christ help you cope with both the rough water and the still water of your life? List three ways.

(1) _____

(2) _____

(3) _____

5. What have you learned, or relearned, today that you could share with a friend?

DAY 69 ━━━━━━━━━━━━━ DATE _____

Turning and Returning

"Bring me back that I may be restored" (Jer. 31:18). "Restore us to Thee, O Lord, that we may be restored" (Lam. 5:21).

Twice Jeremiah uses a most interesting and timely phrase. The best translation of Jeremiah 31:18 and Lamentations 5:21 is: "Cause me [us] to turn in order that I [we] may return."

Here in the midst of Old Testament prophecy is a story of a prodigal son. Ephraim was in a far country. Either by inner rebellion or by the enemy, Ephraim had been taken captive. Behind the captivity lay rebellion, and betrayal. So he cried out: "Cause me to turn in order that I may return" (author's translation).

After proclaiming the miseries of the captivity of God's people, Jeremiah prayed, "Turn us unto thee, O Lord, and we shall be turned" (KJV).

Have you been like the prodigal son with some of your commitments? Perhaps it was that decision to spend a set time each day with God. Or maybe it was a promise to take care of the physical body God gave you with an exercise program of some kind. It could have been that agreement to write friends on a regular basis. Whatever it was, you have now "wandered into a far country" away from the commitment. You need to return.

Do you feel like you're trapped in some type of captivity? Maybe it's a feeling of being trapped in your job or hindered by co-workers or supervisor. Perhaps the whole idea of servanthood is getting a long way off from the original commitment. You need to return.

Jeremiah hit right on target. In order to return to God you must first turn. And only God can cause you to turn. You can't return until you turn.

Reader's Response

A Prayer to Complete

Dear God, "Cause me to turn in order that I may return" to You today. I especially need to turn in regard to . . .

Going Deeper.
1. What were some commitments or goals that you made at the beginning of your hundred days of servanthood?
   (1) _____
   (2) _____
   (3) _____
   (4) _____
2. Which of these commitments have you failed to keep?
3. What would have to happen before God could "turn" you back to the fulfillment of these commitments?
4. What actions could you take to return to these commitments or goals?
   (1) _____
   (2) _____
5. What does it mean to you that, "You can't return until you turn"?

DAY 70 ───────────────── DATE _____
Weep On!

"He saw the city and wept over it" (Luke 19:41).

"Serving the Lord with all humility and with tears" (Acts 20:19).

Be assured of one thing: if Jesus wept over Jerusalem and Paul wept over Ephesus, it's OK for you to weep over your area of service. And weep you will. Oh, the tears may never come out onto your face. They may be inner tears, but tears there will be. It is a part of compassionate, sensitive concern for people (Lam. 2:18-19).

Perhaps you will weep because of the overwhelming task that is before you and the fact that, at your best, you will reach only a few. As Jesus topped the Mount of Olives and looked down on Jerusalem for one of the last times in His earthly life, He wept over the awesome task, and surely it must have seemed to Him to be unfinished. There were so many to reach. Even these who shouted their "Hosannas" on Sunday would shout "Crucify" on Friday.

Or perhaps you will weep like Paul because day in and day out, you will work until you become a part of those whom you serve. Then when you must separate, you will leave a part of yourself with them. Paul asked that the people of Ephesus remember that "for a period of three years I did not cease to admonish each one with tears" (Acts 20:31).

Yes, for whatever the reason you will weep because weeping is a part of service. Perhaps that is why the promise of God is so precious when He promises that some day He will "wipe every tear" from our eyes (Rev. 7:17).

The Bible tells of the weeping of Hagar, Esau, Jacob, the children of Israel, Hannah, Jonathan, David, Saul, Joash, Hezekiah, Peter, Jesus, Paul, and John. You're in good company. Weep on!

Reader's Response

A Prayer to Complete

Father, thank You for making it OK to weep. May my weepings not be too frequent nor too infrequent, and may the compassion that leads to tears be a part of my service today. Right now my weeping is for . . .

Going Deeper

1. What were the circumstances that caused weeping in the two Scripture passages?
   (1) Luke 19:28-44 _____
   (2) Acts 20:17-35 _____
2. Neither Jesus nor Paul seemed the type to weep openly. Why is this true? List some characteristics of each man that made it seem strange that they wept openly. (Or if you feel they were the type to weep openly, list some characteristics of each that lead you to believe this way.)

JESUS	PAUL
(1) _____	(1) _____
(2) _____	(2) _____
(3) _____	(3) _____
(4) _____	(4) _____
(5) _____	(5) _____

3. What were the circumstances surrounding the last time you wept (either outwardly or inwardly)?
4. List two reasons for a person to weep over the situation in your area of service?
   (1) _____
   (2) _____
5. What is one way you can deal creatively with your weeping (inward or outward)?

DAY 71 —————————————— DATE _____
Keep On

"Moses kept right on going; it seemed as though he could see God right there with him" (Heb. 11:27, TLB). "Jesus . . . who for the joy set before Him endured the cross" (Heb. 12:2).

How many servants have there been who have entertained thoughts of quitting before their service is complete? The total number would probably be overwhelming if known. The fact is: most of God's workers have such thoughts from time to time.

No two people in all of history had better reason to quit than did Moses and Jesus. Moses felt the questions of his own call, the guilt of his past sin, the rebellion of his followers, the wrath of God, the discipline of the desert, and the knowledge that he could not himself enter the Land of Promise at the end of the journey. Yet he "kept right on going." There was a reason. He felt God's presence "right there with him."

Jesus would have preferred not to die on the cross. He wrestled with this in Gethsemane. Surely the temptation to leave Jerusalem with the inquisitive Greeks during the last week was a strong temptation. Jesus "endured the cross." Even though He despised its "shame," He kept on. There was a reason. He saw the "joy set before Him."

When you hit the tough spots along the way, take a look at Moses and at Jesus. They made it through by keeping on, and you will too. When those times come, you will see the unseen, you will hear the unheard, you will be touched by the untouchable, and the inner strength of God's indwelling Holy Spirit will sustain you. Keep on!

Reader's Response

A Prayer to Complete

Oh, Spirit of God, strengthen me from within so that when the trials come I will be found worthy. Help me today to keep on . . . and on . . . and on. I need help keeping on in . . .

Going Deeper

1. What are some reasons that could have caused Moses and Jesus to quit?

MOSES		JESUS	
(1)	_____	(1)	_____
(2)	_____	(2)	_____
(3)	_____	(3)	_____
(4)	_____	(4)	_____

2. What are some reasons you've had to quit?
   (1) _____
   (2) _____
   (3) _____
   (4) _____

3. How do your reasons compare to those of Moses and Jesus?

4. What are two things that have enabled you to "endure" and "keep on"?
   (1) _____
   (2) _____

5. How will your ability to "keep on" serve you in the future?

DAY 72 ━━━━━━━━━━━━━━ DATE _____

Reap On

"Whatever a man sows, this he will also reap. . . . And let us not lose heart in doing good, for in due time we shall reap if we do not grow weary" (Gal. 6:7,9).

The time for reporting results is drawing near. What will you have to tell? They're going to ask, you know. Folks will want to know. However you choose to word it, you will tell them you reaped that which was sown.

Paul set forth this life principle for us: that which is sown equals that which is reaped. You may reap of that which you did not sow. Jesus indicated that some people do (Matt. 25:26). You may reap later, or someone else may reap later, that which you have sown (John 4:37-38). But that which is planted is that which will grow.

There is an easy way of explaining the lack of results that many servants fall victim to occasionally. When you have tried to explain the lack of results, you may be tempted to add, "But I sowed a lot of seed." That's good, and folks will be proud of you for that, but read John 4:36 very carefully. It is both "he who sows and he who reaps" that rejoice together, but only "he who reaps" is mentioned as "receiving wages." Don't read more into this than is meant to be there, but do read that it is extremely important to reap.

In your eagerness to sow seed in these days of service, don't overlook the reaping of some ripe seed. Remember, Jesus did not say, "Look on the fields that are ready to be sown," but, "Look on the fields, that they are white for harvest" (v. 35).

Do not lose heart in doing good. If you do not grow weary you will, in due time, reap. Reap on!

Reader's Response

A Prayer to Complete

God of the harvest, lift up my weary eyes to see the necessity of reaping Your harvest. As I sow today, make me aware of opportunities to reap related to . . .

Going Deeper

1. List four attempts to sow seed during your hundred days of service.

   (1) _____

   (2) _____

   (3) _____

   (4) _____

2. In which of the above attempts did you or someone else reap a spiritual harvest?

3. Which of your seed-sowing attempts are you willing to leave for someone else to reap?
4. What do you think Jesus meant to say in John 4:36 when He said only the one who reaps receives wages?
5. What are two areas where you could reap a harvest before your hundred days of service are over?

(1) _____

(2) _____

DAY 73 ——————————————— DATE ——————————

Sleep On

"The sleep of the working man is pleasant" (Eccl. 5:12). "Sleep on now, and take your rest" (Mark 14:41, KJV).

It was to be for them one of the most exciting and best remembered nights of their lives. It was the last night of Jesus on this earth during His earthly ministry. They had been asked to pray *with* Him. Oh, what a privilege! Not asked to pray *for* Him nor even *to* Him, but *with* Him. Judas and the soldiers were coming with swords and clubs to take Him. This was the night of preparation. The prayers of this night would ensure the success of the cross. And the disciples fell asleep!

Have you hit a very strategic time in your service when the task called for the best you had in you only to find yourself sleepy? Have you wanted very much to awaken on a given day to meet the excitement of the day with gusto only to find that the lateness of the bedtime hour on the preceeding night prevented you from doing so? Have you needed very much to pay attention to what someone was saying only to find the lack of sleep caused your mind to wander?

This last week of Jesus' earthly life had been a hectic time, and the pace must have been intense, but surely these disciples could have found a better time to sleep. It would have been far easier for these disciples to have stayed awake in the crucial

140

time had they gotten the necessary sleep at its proper time. Sometimes the most crucial thing you can do is sleep. Then when the Lord says to you "Arise, let us be going" (Mark 14:42), not only will your mind and heart be ready but so will your body.

It might aid sleep to know that while you sleep, "He who keeps you will not slumber" (Ps. 121:3). Sleep is a part of God's plan for your ministry. "For God has not destined us for wrath, but for obtaining salvation through our Lord Jesus Christ, who died for us, that whether we are awake or asleep, we may live together with Him" (1 Thess. 5:9-10). Sleep on!

Reader's Response

A Prayer to Complete

Father, You must have known *all* about us when You made us in your image. You rested only on the seventh day. Help me to rest every day and stop trying to play God. I need rest tonight because . . .

Going Deeper

1. From Mark 14:32-42 list some reasons why the disciples should have stayed awake.

   (1) _____
   (2) _____
   (3) _____
   (4) _____

2. What could the disciples have done to have been better prepared for this night?

3. Can you think of a recent experience where a lack of proper sleep prevented you from doing your best?

4. React to the statement: "Sometimes the most crucial thing you can do is sleep."

5. Of what significance is it to you to know that God does not sleep (Ps. 121:3)?

DAY 74 ━━━━━━━━━━━━━ DATE ━━━━━━━━━

When You Get to the Jumping-Off Point . . . Stand!

"I will stand . . ./I will keep watch . . ./Record the vision" (Hab. 2:1-2).

One can often tell the real conditions of a given situation by the words used to describe it. Look at the words used by Habakkuk to describe his situation: *violence, iniquity, wickedness, destruction, strife, contention* (1:2-3). He also said, "Law is ignored/ And justice is never upheld,/For the wicked surround the righteous;/Therefore, justice comes out perverted" (v. 4).

What does one do in a situation like that? It was a real jumping-off point. Habakkuk first asked some questions of God: "Why art Thou silent when the wicked swallowed up/ those more righteous than they?/Why hast Thou made men like the fish of the sea?" (vv. 13-14).

Have you hit upon similar days and situations? Have you reached the end of the road and been ready to jump? Have you been ready to ask some questions of God concerning the conditions in your situtation? What will you do then? Do what Habakkuk did!

Habakkuk said, "I will stand on my guard post" (2:1). Having thought of everything else to do, stand firm. Hold your position. Remain where God put you. The temptation is to give up and go home. The challenge is to "stand."

Habakkuk also said he would "keep watch to see what He will speak to me" (2:1). He knew God would speak, and so do you. It is not your job to determine if God will speak or not in a given situation, but it is your job to listen so that you may hear when He does speak.

When the Lord did speak, He instructed Habakkuk to "Record the vision" (2:2) which implies the vision was to be shared. Your assignment is to share the vision of God. He may need to renew it in your life as He did with Habakkuk, but it must be shared.

Whatever your situation, "stand," "keep watch," and "record the vision."

Reader's Response

A Prayer to Complete

Father, I don't always understand the situation around me, and I sometimes want to question Your reasons for doing things, but down deep I really want to "stand" and "keep watch" and "record the vision." Help me to be true to this desire today as I . . .

Going Deeper

1. What three words would you use to describe your service opportunities?
   (1) _____
   (2) _____
   (3) _____
2. How do your words compare to those used by Habakkuk?
3. Did you reach any points during your hundred days of service where you felt like you were at the "jumping-off point"? What did you do?
4. How have you fulfilled the following in your service?
   (1) Stand _____
   (2) Keep watch _____
   (3) Record the vision _____
5. The writer says, "Your assignment is to share the vision of God." How can you do this?

DAY 75 ———————————— DATE _____

When the Old Gives Way to the New

"If any man is in Christ, he is a new creature; the old things passed away; behold, new things have come" (2 Cor. 5:17).

He shook my hand at the airport and introduced himself.

Dressed in cowboy boots and faded jeans, he was to be my transportation for the weekend. As we rode to the hotel, my new friend unfolded his story. His marriage had failed, the results of a recent knee surgery were yet to be tested, and he was broke. On his way to ride in a rodeo, his truck broke down in front of a Baptist church in a Midwest city on Saturday night. Sunday morning he went to church for the first time in years and met Jesus right where he had last experienced Him. Monday morning a new cowboy sold his trailer and his horse, got a job in a local hospital, rented a room, and began to witness to the down-and-out and the hurting people of a city. He had become a new creature in Christ.

We all have those broken-down experiences in our lives. Some break physically, some emotionally, some mentally, others socially, and still others spiritually. As we heal from our various brokenesses, it is refreshing to know, "the old things passed away; behold, new things have come."

You are a new creature in Christ. Live in the newness of Christlikeness.

Reader's Response

A Prayer to Complete

God of creation and recreation, just as the old has passed away, help me today to pass on Your newness, especially as I
. . .

Going Deeper
1. Have you had a broken-down experience in your life recently? If so, describe it.
2. How did you find healing for your brokenness?
3. What are some "old things" that have "passed away" in your life"?
   (1) _____
   (2) _____

(3) _____

4. List some of the "new things" that "have come" into your life.

(1) _____
(2) _____
(3) _____
(4) _____

5. What does it mean to you to "live in the newness of Christ-likeness"?

Day 76 ———————————— Date _____
Who Is He?

"Who is this?" (Luke 5:21; 7:49; Mark 4:41; Luke 9:9; Matt. 21:10).

You will face many questions during your days of service. Some will be crucial. Others will be crucial only to the one asking the question. Some you will answer. Others you will ask of wiser persons before answering. Some you will ignore. One question must not be ignored, for it is extremely crucial. You will face it, and you will, in some way, answer it. The question: Who is He?

Jesus first faced the question after healing a paralytic who had been lowered into Jesus' presence through a hole in the roof. It was the scribes and Pharisees who first voiced the question. As they reasoned among themselves they asked, "Who is this man who speaks blasphemies?" (Luke 5:21).

Shortly thereafter, Jesus accepted an invitation to dine at the home of Simon, a Pharisee. After the meal, a woman, known to those present as a sinful woman, entered and began to wash Jesus' feet with her tears and dry his feet with her hair. Jesus forgave her of her sins to which the guests asked, "Who is this man who even forgives sins?" (Luke 7:49).

Again, after stilling a storm, the disciples who were in the boat with Him asked, "Who then is this, that even the wind and the sea obey Him?" (Mark 4:41). His deeds caused Herod to ask, "Who is this man about whom I hear such things?" (Luke 9:9).

At Jesus' triumphant entry, Matthew tells us that "the city [of Jerusalem] was stirred, saying, 'Who is this?' " (Matt. 21: 10). And Jesus asked His disciples, "Who do people say that the Son of Man is?" (Matt. 16:13). And again, "Who do you say that I am?" (Matt. 16:15).

When you have shared all you have read and heard to this question, the final answer must come from who Jesus is to you personally. So again, the question, this time to you is: Who is He?

Reader's Response

A Prayer to Complete

Lord, help me to answer in my own experience again and again who You are and having done so, may I have boldness to tell someone today. I would like to tell people that You are
. . .

Going Deeper

1. Read the Scripture accounts that are background for today's material and state the reason why each group inquired as to who Jesus was:
   (1) Luke 5:17-26 _____
   (2) Luke 7:36-50 _____
   (3) Mark 4:35-41 _____
   (4) Luke 9:1-9_____
   (5) Matthew 21:1-11_____
   (6) Matthew 16:13-14 _____
2. What are some reasons today why people would inquire as to the identity of Jesus?
   (1) _____

  (2) _____
  (3) _____
  (4) _____
  (5) _____

3. How can you minister to the above reasons why people today seek to understand who Jesus is?

4. Why do you think Jesus asked His disciples who they thought He was (Matt. 16:15)?

5. What were some of the responses given to the questions of who Jesus was?
  (1) Luke 5:17-26 _____
  (2) Luke 7:36-50 _____
  (3) Mark 4:35-41 _____
  (4) Luke 9:1-9 _____
  (5) Matthew 21:1-11 _____
  (6) Matthew 16:13-14 _____

DAY 77 ————————————— DATE _____

The Life-Bread

"I am the bread of life" (John 6:35,48).

To help you better understand who He was and is, Jesus gave a series of self-descriptions. These "I ams" of Jesus are recorded in the Gospel of John. It will help you explain who He is when you know some of the ways Jesus described Himself.

The day following the miraculous feeding of the multitude, the crowds found Jesus again. Immediately, Jesus perceived that their true intent was to be fed. Contrasting their life with the life of a believer, Jesus exclaimed to them twice, "I am the bread of life (John 6:35,48).

They asked for a sign and brought out that Moses had provided manna in the wilderness for their ancestors. Jesus explained His superiority to manna in terms of quality. "He who comes to Me shall not hunger" (v. 35). The quality of Jesus as bread is that He meets every need and satisfies every desire. Nothing else can do this. Jesus further explained His superiority to manna in terms of quantity. "I am the living bread that came down out of heaven; if anyone eats of this bread, he shall live forever; and the bread also which I shall give for the life of the world is My flesh" (v. 51). There is enough of Jesus as bread for every person in the world. His bread is not just for the day's needs nor just for one nation but for every need in every life.

But telling you to feed on Jesus is like putting a small child in a vegetable garden and telling him to eat. You are as overwhelmed and inadequate as that small child in the garden. God knew that. So Jesus came "down out of heaven" and allowed His body to be broken, so you could begin to feed on Him. It is only through a personal relationship with the Life-Bread, Jesus Christ, that you can be fed and grow as a believer.

Reader's Response

A Prayer to Complete

Lord, may I feed on You and You alone today as I encounter You in Your Word and in Your world. May this be a day of growth as I share You with . . .

Going Deeper

1. In what ways have you observed the spiritual hunger among people recently?

    (1) _____

    (2) _____

    (3) _____

    (4) _____

2. How do these ways compare to the ways you might find in other places?

3. List the names of two persons you know who are spiritually hungry.

148

(1) _____
(2) _____
4. How could you share Jesus, the Life-Bread, with them?
5. What are three ways you have grown and matured during these hundred days as a result of learning more about Jesus?
    (1) _____
    (2) _____
    (3) _____

DAY 78 ——————————— DATE _____
The Light

"I am the light of the world" (John 8:12).

This scene takes place in the court of the women of the Temple. Located in this area were the large golden lampstands. On each night of the Feast of Tabernacles these were lit and shed their brilliant light over the Temple and the city. It was now the end of the week of the Feast and the lights had been extinguished. Some interpreters feel that it was in response to the contrast of the darkness that Jesus said, "I am the light of the world; he who follows Me shall not walk in the darkness, but shall have the light of life" (John 8:12).

Preceeding this self-description, Jesus had encountered a group of scribes and Pharisees who had brought to Him a woman who had been caught in the act of adultery. They demanded that Jesus endorse their stoning of the woman in keeping with the law of Moses. This encounter serves as a backdrop for the meaning of Jesus' self-description.

These religious leaders were really not concerned with the woman or the Law, but were trying to trap Jesus into contradicting Himself and His ministry. Jesus saw through their reasons, and, like light, He penetrated to the real.

Not only does light penetrate, but it also destroys the darkness. The two cannot coexist. The religious leaders saw only sin, darkness, in the woman caught in adultery. Jesus saw past her sin, and, like light, He destroyed this darkness.

In addition to these, light illumines that which is around it. After Jesus had destroyed the darkness of sin in her life, He illumined it by saying to her, "Go your way; from now on sin no more" (v. 11).

Jesus, knowing that God's plan was for us to be "like Him" told His disciples, "You are the light of the world" (Matt. 5:14). The qualities of His Light must become the qualities of our lives.

Reader's Response

A Prayer to Complete

Lord of light, reflect off me. Let my light so shine that others will see my good works and glorify the Father in heaven. May this happen today as I . . .

Going Deeper

1. What evidences of darkness have you experienced recently?
   (1) _____
   (2) _____
   (3) _____
2. How have you seen Jesus illumine this darkness?
3. How is the darkness in the world in comparison to the darkness you've seen recently?
4. What are two ways you can reflect Jesus, the Light, in your area of service?
   (1) _____
   (2) _____
5. How have "the qualities of His Light" become "the qualities of your life"?

DAY 79 ————————————— DATE _____

The Good Shepherd

"I am the good shepherd" (John 10:11).

Here Jesus likens Himself to the quite honorable profession of the shepherd. In the Bible, God is often referred to as the Shepherd of Israel. Isaiah 40, Psalm 23, and Revelation 7 contain beautiful references to the shepherd. It is the purpose of Jesus to show the contrast between the true, Good Shepherd and the false, evil shepherd as well as to show the attitude of the sheep toward their shepherd.

The occasion for this self-description follows a conversation between Jesus and the Pharisees in the preceeding chapter. They were trying to assert themselves on the basis that they, not Jesus, were the rightful leaders of the people. Furthermore, the Pharisees presented Jesus as a false leader and an outsider (John 9:18-34).

When Jesus, by contrast, referred to Himself as the Good Shepherd, He was not meaning kind or gracious but real and true. He was not false like the thief and the hireling—or even the Pharisees.

The Good Shepherd knows His sheep, and He "calls his own sheep by name" (John 10:3). The shepherd in biblical times knew each particular trait of each sheep. So the Good Shepherd knows all about His sheep.

The Good Shepherd can be trusted to lead His sheep in the right way. New Testament shepherds led their sheep by their voice, and the sheep would follow no other voice. So Jesus leads us where we ought to go (John 10:4-5).

To follow the Good Shepherd meant life. Shepherds of those days cared for their sheep whereas "the thief comes only to steal, and kill, and destroy" (v. 10). Jesus came that they and we might "have life, and might have it abundantly" (v. 10).

Finally, the Good Shepherd, in contrast to the hireling (v. 12), "lays down His life for the sheep" (v. 11). In the midst of many voices, we must follow and urge others to follow the true Shepherd, Jesus Christ.

Reader's Response

A Prayer to Complete

Lord, we are indeed like sheep. Forgive us when we wander astray. Welcome us back into the fold, and may we return not only forgiven but bringing other sheep with us. Help me today as I . . .

Going Deeper

1. In what ways have you felt like a sheep who has been led by the Good Shepherd?
   (1) _____
   (2) _____
   (3) _____
2. Do you know any sheep that are not yet in the "fold" of the Good Shepherd? What could you do to invite these to come into the "fold"?
3. John 10:19-21 says a division arose among the people because of the claims of Jesus. Have you seen a division among the "religious people"? What was the result? How could the negative aspects of the division have been avoided?
4. Are you anxious to get back to the sheepfold when you are away from it? If so, why?
5. How can you do a better job of presenting Jesus as the Good Shepherd?

DAY 80 ———————————— DATE _____
The Resurrection and the Life
"I am the resurrection and the life" (John 11:25).
The setting was Bethany. Jesus had arrived to find Mary and

Martha mourning the death of their brother Lazarus. To these sorrowing sisters in the presence of death itself, Jesus announced that He was "the resurrection and the life" and stated that "he who believes in Me shall live even if he dies" (11:25).

Preceeding that self-description of life and purpose, Martha had attempted to limit Jesus. Before being too hard on Martha, perhaps we ought to look at the limitations which we try to impose on Jesus.

Martha tried to limit Jesus in regard to space. She said, "Lord, if You had been here, my brother would not have died" (v. 21). Jesus did not have to be visibly present in order for Lazarus to live. Have you tried to limit God with regard to space in your life? Perhaps it was no more than the question: "Lord, where are you?"

Martha tried also to limit Jesus in regard to time. Jesus responded to her first attempt at limitation by assuring her that Lazarus would live. To this she responded, "I know that he will rise again in the resurrection on the last day" (v. 24). Jesus did not have to wait for "the last day" to resurrect Lazarus. Have you tried to limit God with regard to time in your life? Perhaps it was no more than the question: "Lord, when?"

In the midst of our attempts to place limits on God, we need to hear Jesus say to us, "I am the resurrection and the life." He is beyond our limitations of space and time.

Having realized this, we are ready to hear the rest of what Jesus said, "He who believes in Me shall live even if he dies" (v. 25).

Reader's Response

A Prayer to Complete
Lord, forgive our feeble attempts to place limitations on You. Teach us again that You are above and beyond, and our task deals not with limitations but with life. May I learn again today as I . . .

Going Deeper

1. Have you tried to place any space limitations on Jesus recently? If so, what did you learn from the experience?
2. Have you tried to place any time limitations on Jesus recently? If so, what did you learn from the experience?
3. In what ways do people where you serve try to limit Jesus?
   (1) _____
   (2) _____
   (3) _____
   (4) _____
4. How can you share the message that Jesus is the "life" with those whom you serve?
5. React to the feeling that "our task deals not with limitations but with life."

DAY 81 ━━━━━━━━━━━━━━ DATE _____
The Way, the Truth, the Life

"I am the way, and the truth, and the life" (John 14:6).

Into one statement Jesus included three self-descriptions. It was His last will and testament to His disciples. His death was near. Following His beautiful statement of beginning, "Let not your heart be troubled. . . . I go to prepare a place for you. . . . I will come again . . . that where I am, there you may be also" (14:1-3). Thomas asked, "Lord, we do not know where You are going; how do we know the way?" (v. 5). Jesus addressed Himself to the question of Thomas with this threefold self-description.

The true value of a way is not realized until one has followed it through the unknown. It was the unknown about which Jesus spoke and Thomas questioned. Jesus comforted Thomas and others by establishing Himself as the known way by which we would journey. You will never go into a situation with Jesus but that Jesus will also be the way through and out.

No one is ever lost on the journey who knows and follows Jesus.

From the beginning of time, people have sought for truth. Some have suffered and died in its pursuit. Millions have been spent on the search. But God, who is the source of our urge to discover truth, sent His only Son to announce to a world of searchers, "I am the truth." The falsehood of any person or idea will disappear as he or it draws near to Jesus, the Truth.

It was not until later that the disciples fully understood the third self-description of Jesus in this statement. His resurrection made all the difference. Earthly life is enriched and made meaningful in the knowledge that when evil has done its worst, there is still life in Him.

Having made three bold descriptions of Himself, Jesus made one more bold statement, "No one comes to the Father, but through Me" (v. 6). This is our solution and our challenge to share with others.

Reader's Response

A Prayer to Complete

Father, thank You for the bold claim of Your Son to be "the way, the truth, and the life." May I catch that boldness as I minister in Your name today in the midst of . . .

Going Deeper

1. What has been your experience with Jesus in the following relationships?
   (1) As the way _____
   (2) As the truth _____
   (3) As the life_____
2. Have you been privileged to share "the way" with some non-Christian? What was the result?
3. In what ways do people whom you serve search for the way, the truth, and the life?

(1) _____
(2) _____
(3) _____
(4) _____
(5) _____

4. How can you help them in their search?

5. Since the "truth" makes you free (John 8:32) and Jesus is the "truth" (14:6), what feelings of freedom have you experienced recently? What difference will these feelings make in your future attempts at service?

DAY 82 ━━━━━━━━━━━━ DATE _____

If You Will . . . Then You Shall Be

"If you will indeed obey My voice and keep My covenant, then you shall be My own possession among all the peoples, for all the earth is Mine; and you shall be to Me a kingdom of priests and a holy nation" (Ex. 19:5-6).

God did not say, "If you will . . . I will." He did say, "If you will . . . you shall be." He has already set forth for us His standards, His covenant. As we obey what we already know to be His leadership, we can expect to be seen in special ways by God.

He calls His special people by a Hebrew word *segullah*. It is used only eight times in the Old Testament. In those days a king owned everything in his territory. All buildings were his. All land, all coins, everything belonged to the king. Owning everything left little room for personal satisfaction. So in the palace of a king there would be a treasure chest of his own special possessions, precious stones, and other collections. This special collection was called *segullah*. God said, "If you will obey My voice and keep My Covenant, then you shall be My *segullah*." All things belong to God, but we are His special possession "among all the peoples." In Malachi the word appears again, " 'They will be Mine,' says the Lord of hosts, on the day that I prepare My own possession" (3:17).

But there is responsibility. He also calls us His "kingdom of priests." Using this phrase only once in the Old Testament, God sets forth our ministry as one of intercessory priesthood on behalf of the nations. Finally, He says we shall be "a holy nation." We are to be set apart like a holy day or a holy place is set apart—set apart so we can minister to the nations. Our privilege is matched only by our responsibility.

Reader's Response

A Prayer to Complete

Lord God, may I see my responsibility to minister in light of my special relationship to You. I pray that it will make a difference today as I work in . . .

Going Deeper

1. In what ways did you obey God's leadership related to your hundred days of service?

   (1) _____
   (2) _____
   (3) _____

2. The writer says, "As we obey what we already know to be His leadership, we can expect to be seen in special ways by God." How do you think God saw you at the beginning of your hundred days of service?

3. How do you think God sees you now?

4. If you are God's special possession, what do you see as your corresponding responsibility?

5. For what purposes has God set you apart?

   (1) _____
   (2) _____
   (3) _____

DAY 83 ———————————————— DATE ——————————
Problems or Potential?

"He saw a great multitude and He felt compassion for them because they were like sheep without a shepherd" (Mark 6:34).

For over an hour he had sat silently with arms crossed in front of his chest while the others present discussed how to train persons to witness. I worry about people like him. I worry about what they are thinking. After an hour of worry, he let me know his thoughts with one statement, "How can you hope to train persons to witness when they have so many problems!"

My response was too harsh, but it came out before much thought, "Jesus had problems. I can name you twelve of them who followed Him around. Problems didn't stop Him from witnessing." Sure persons have problems. Everyone has problems. Problems do not become a problem until they are all you can see. Then you have a real problem.

Do you remember the children's poem about the pussy cat who went to England to see the queen, and all that stupid cat saw was a mouse under the queen's throne? What you are determines to a great degree what you see. The cat saw a mouse because that's the way cats are. Problem-oriented people are going to see problems.

It is important for children of God to remember who they are and, in spite of their problems, to allow who they are in Christ to determine what they see. Don't see problems, see potential! The disciples saw people like sheep. Jesus saw sheep that needed a shepherd.

Keep lifting up your eyes. You are a child of the King.

Reader's Response

A Prayer to Complete

Lord, may I not get so involved in my own problems that I fail to see the potential in those around me, especially

Going Deeper

1. List three problems that you are currently having in your life:
   (1) _____
   (2) _____
   (3) _____

2. How do you feel about the statement, "Problems do not become a problem until they are all you can see"?

3. List three "potentials" out of the three problems you listed above:
   (1) _____
   (2) _____
   (3) _____

4. How can who you are in Christ determine what you see?

5. In Mark 6, what did Jesus do when He saw people like sheep without a shepherd? What application does that have to you as you see people today?

DAY 84 ———————————————— DATE _____

Focused Vision

"Where there is no vision, the people perish" (Prov. 29:18, KJV).

A recent trip to the eye doctor brought to remembrance that vision is not good of itself. Vision must be focused to be effective. Some are fortunate enough to have perfect physical vision. Few, if any, have perfect spiritual vision. We need to allow God to focus our vision.

Spiritual vision needs to focus, if only briefly, on the past. We are a part of what and who we have met. Many persons and events have shaped our lives. We need to focus just long enough to learn. We can live off the past but not in the past. In a real sense our past has brought us to the present so that God can take us further. "Son of man, see with your eyes, hear with your ears, and give attention to all that I am going to show you; for you have been brought here in order to show it to you" (Ezek. 40:4).

Spiritual vision needs also to focus on the present, "forgetting what lies behind and reaching forward to what lies ahead" (Phil. 3:13). Without getting too entrenched in the past or too excited about the future, we need to "work the works of Him who sent me, as long as it is day" (John 9:4).

Spiritual vision must also focus on the future. Similar to the way God instructed Isaiah to "enlarge the place of your tent" (Isa. 54:2), we need to prepare for God's future. It is far easier to serve without considering the future tense of vision for then we can make our own plans. But our God is the God of the future as well as of the past and present (Heb. 13:8).

Today is your day of service. To be farsighted or nearsighted is to miss seeing clearly what God has for you today.

Reader's Response

A Prayer to Complete

Focus my vision right now, Lord. Give me the proper appreciation of the past. Teach me from my past. Give me a faith vision of the future. But help me to work today. I specifically request your help as I try to envision . . .

Going Deeper

1. List three descriptive words that show how you see your past experiences.

   (1) _____

   (2) _____

   (3) _____

2. List three descriptive words that show how you see your present position or condition.

   (1) _____

   (2) _____

(3) _____

3. List three descriptive words that show your future vision for your Christian service.

   (1) _____
   (2) _____
   (3) _____

4. Can you see any progression in your vision? If so, what?

5. "To be farsighted or nearsighted is to miss seeing clearly what God has for you today." What does God have for you today?

DAY 85 ———————————— DATE _____
Looking Back

"The time of my departure has come" (2 Tim. 4:6).

As Paul neared the end of his missionary career, he had the opportunity, because of Roman imprisonment, to look back over his ministry. In one of his last writings he described to Timothy how he viewed his life.

Paul's life was a conflict or fight. "I have fought the good fight," wrote Paul (2 Tim. 4:7). His life from the time of his conversion to Christ had been one of sacrifice, toil, self-denial, peril, persecution, and even poverty. He had traveled without the comfort of a home or the warmth of a family. He had survived the dangers of land and sea. He had been beaten in public. And often Paul was alone.

Paul also viewed life as a race to be run. He wrote, "I have finished the course" (v. 7). The allusion was no doubt to the Grecian games of his day. His was not a wasted race as some men run. Nor was Paul's a race marked by wickedness or hopelessness. His was a race run with patience and pride with eyes always on the goal.

Finally, Paul viewed life as something to be kept. He wrote, "I have kept the faith" (v. 7). He had given up much to obtain the faith. He was already a leader in his world when he was converted to Christianity. He already possessed honor among his countrymen and respect among his peers. But he chose Christ, and he was not about to give that up. So Paul looked back at his life as a fight fought, a race run, and a faith kept. Then Paul looked forward to his "crown of righteousness" (v. 8).

As you approach the end of your hundred days of service, yours will be a time of looking back. Your ministry is not over as was Paul's, but this time is no less a time of reflection on the past. How does your past look from this perspective?

Reader's Response

A Prayer to Complete

Thank you, Lord, for bringing me to this point from which I can look back on my experiences. As I reflect, may I continue to serve those around me even as I give thanks for . . .

Going Deeper

1. Do you see any parallel to the way Paul looked back on his ministry and the way you look back on yours? If so, list the parallels.

    (1) _____

    (2) _____

    (3) _____

    (4) _____

2. How have you

    (1) Fought the fight _____

    (2) Run the race_____

    (3) Kept the faith _____

3. "How does your past look from this perspective?"

4. In what ways did you see God working during the hundred days in your field of service?

    (1) _____

(2) _____
(3) _____

5. In what ways did you experience God working in your own life during your hundred days of service?
    (1) _____
    (2) _____
    (3) _____

DAY 86 ──────────────── DATE _____
Looking Forward

"In the future" (2 Tim. 4:8).

The "future" about which Paul wrote was an eternity spent with his Lord. His "crown of righteousness" was a crown of victory similar to the winner's crown in a race. "That day" of which he wrote was the day of judgment and reward (2 Tim. 4:8).

Your "future" is different. Yours is a return to the daily routine and the friendship of peers. Your "crown" is the knowledge of a task completed. This segment of your race has been run. Your "day" is a time of reward and the beginning of a new chapter in your life.

Several sobering suggestions are in order. Some will not be as appreciative of your work as you think they ought to be. They will ask, "How was your experience of service?" Then they will not really listen as you tell them.

Response will be enough for some when you say, "My experience was fine," or "It was a growing experience." Their interest stops short of wanting to hear the details.

Others will not know what a servant really is, and for that reason they will not be concerned about hearing your story. They still need to hear, for some of them will want to try a hundred days of servanthood.

As you look forward, do not be filled with false expectations.

The coming adjustment to the routine may be more difficult than the past adjustment to your service. You may not experience the approval and applause of persons.

Paul fought his fight and ran his race not for the approval or even for the applause of the crowd but for the glory of God. He kept the faith, knowing that some could care less, and others just didn't understand. But he did all for God. And so do you. Don't you?

Reader's Response

A Prayer to Complete

God help me adjust to my future. Give me the assurance that You will be there just as real as you have been in the past. Thank You for friends. Help me to understand and minister to . . .

Going Deeper

1. How will your experiences of these hundred days be translated into your life-style in the future?

    (1) _____

    (2) _____

    (3) _____

    (4) _____

2. What differences will your servant activities make within your family?

    (1) _____

    (2) _____

3. Does it bother you that "Some will not be as appreciative of your work as you think they ought to be"? How will you cope with this?

4. What adjustments back to your routine do you anticipate?

    (1) _____

    (2) _____

    (3) _____

5. How will lessons learned during these hundred days help you through the above adjustments?

DAY 87 ————————————— DATE _____
The Call of God: How Long?

"Lord, how long?" (Isa. 6:11).

"God has called me to give up three months for his service." That's what the missionary said in his testimony, but was he right? How many times in the Bible does God call a person and put a time limit on the call? We do that, not God.

God called Abraham to "Go forth from your country" and promised to make of him "a great nation" (Gen. 12:1-2), but no time limit was mentioned. God called Moses from the burning bush, "Come now, and I will send you to Pharoah, so that you may bring My people, the sons of Israel, out of Egypt" (Ex. 3:10). Again, no time limit.

Samuel responded to God's call with, "Speak, for Thy servant is listening (1 Sam. 3:10). God spoke to Samuel, but no time limit was mentioned. God called Amos to, "Go prophesy to My people Israel" (Amos 7:15), but no time limit was mentioned.

The hundred days is only a part of your overall call from God. The calling does not terminate with a hundred days but continues. Because of the experiences of these hundred days you are better prepared to hear the next phase of your calling.

How long, Lord? Until, "These will wage war against the Lamb, and the Lamb will overcome them, because He is Lord of lords and King of kings, and those who are with Him are the called and chosen and faithful" (Rev. 17:14).

Reader's Response

A Prayer to Complete
Lord, thank You that Your call is not temporal but continual. May I work today in the security of Your call, and may I look with anticipation to Your continuing movement in my life which I interpret to be . . .

Going Deeper
1. List one characteristic of God from each of the following passages of Scripture.
   (1) Genesis 12:1-3 _____
   (2) Exodus 3:1-14 _____
   (3) 1 Samuel 3:1-14 _____
   (4) Amos 7:10-17 _____
2. Which of the above characteristics (or other characteristics) have you experienced in your relationship to God?
   (1) _____
   (2) _____
3. Of what significance is the Revelation 17:14 reference to the length of God's call to His people?
4. What has God communicated of His will to you?
5. Respond to the statement: "Because of the experiences of these hundred days, you are better prepared to hear the next phase of your calling."
6. How do you interpret the "next phase of *your* calling" at this time in your experience?

DAY 88 ——————————————— DATE _____
God's Second Call

"The word of the Lord came to Jonah the second time" (Jonah 3:1).

Has God ever had to extend to you a second call? He communicated to you a job that needed to be done or an attitude that needed to be adjusted or a relationship that needed to be worked on, and you heard the communication, but somehow as time went by, you let it slip out of your thoughts. In some way you ran from the call.

Your story would sound familiar to Jonah. God called him to go to Nineveh and preach to the people that they were displeasing God. But the Bible says, "Jonah rose up to flee to Tarshish from the presence of the Lord" (1:3). After a trip in a fishing boat and trip inside a fish, Jonah was ready to hear God's second call. And it came.

"Now the word of the Lord came to Jonah the second time, saying, 'Arise, go to Nineveh' " (3:1-2). This time Jonah "arose and went to Nineveh according to the word of the Lord" (v. 3).

As you run from God's first call, there comes a time in your life for interruption. God has a way of slowing you down and putting you in a place where you can hear His second call. I trust for you it will not be as drastic as it was for Jonah, but God has no limits in where He puts those whom He is calling.

Perhaps your current place of service is just such a place, and this is just such a time. Listen very closely. God may be calling.
Reader's Response

A Prayer to Complete

O Lord, if you are trying to communicate with me, may I have ears to hear today. Speak to me as I . . .

Going Deeper
1. Have you ever experienced a "call" from God? If so, describe it.
2. What has been your recent relationship to the above call?
3. If God extended to you a "second call," what do you think it would be?
4. What kind of call would God issue to you in relation to your present place of service?
5. What actions could you take to ensure that you will always be sensitive to God's call to you?

    (1) _____
    (2) _____
    (3) _____
    (4) _____
    (5) _____

DAY 89 ━━━━━━━━━━━━━━━ DATE _____
Living on Top of Circumstances

"My circumstances have turned out for the greater progress of the gospel" (Phil. 1:12).

Paul was in prison, and it appeared that the gospel's advance would be greatly hindered. According to Paul, this was not the case. For month after month no missionary journey was made, no sea was crossed, no highway was traveled, no new city was entered. In it's place was the monotony of prison life.

Paul referred to "my circumstances." Look at his circumstances three years in exile in Arabia; disagreement with Barnabas resulting in their split up; arrested, beaten, and jailed for preaching; placed under a vow to be killed; enduring a shipwreck at sea; and imprisonment in Rome. Yet these "circumstances . . . turned out for the greater progress of the gospel."

Circumstances cause some to bow their head in defeat and

say, "What must be, must be." But others see only hope and turn circumstances into progress.

Life with God is like a surprise party. Paul was confronted with a surprise. What looked like the end of his ministry turned out to be one of God's surprises. Paul's liabilities became assets. His frustrations became fulfillments. His imprisonment did not close doors; it opened doors. Paul lived on top of his circumstances.

Your circumstances during these hundred days have either gotten the best of you, or you've lived on top of them. They have either been stumbling blocks or stepping-stones to "the greater progress of the gospel."

Paul had written to the Christians of Rome, "God causes all things to work together for good to those who love God, to those who are called according to His purpose" (Rom. 8:28). Now he was living out his statement in the prison of their city.

Reader's Response

A Prayer to Complete

Lord, help me to live on top of my circumstances like You and Paul did. Today I need to live on top of . . .

Going Deeper

1. According to Philippians 1:13-14, what were two results of Paul living on top of his circumstances?

    (1) _____

    (2) _____

2. What were three "circumstances" that could have hindered the advance of the gospel in your hundred days of service?

    (1) _____

    (2) _____

    (3) _____

3. How did you live (or fail to live) on top of the above "circumstances"?

(1) _____

(2) _____

(3) _____

4. How do you react to the feeling that "Life with God is like a surprise party"?

5. What action can you take that would enable you to live on top of your circumstances today?

Mixed Motivation

"The wishing is present in me, but the doing of the good is not" (Rom. 7:18).

Out of his confusion, Paul wrote, "For that which I am doing, I do not understand; for I am not practicing what I would like to do, but I am doing the very thing I hate" (Rom. 7:15). After further discussion of his problems, Paul exclaimed, "Wretched man that I am!" (v. 24). Can you identify with Paul?

Your schedule, pace, daily priorities, environment, and peers change. You'd like to keep up the pace of your past, but circumstances won't let you.

Maybe you need to learn what Paul learned in prison, "It is God who is at work in you, both to will and to work for His good pleasure" (Phil. 2:13). Before salvation, Christ works on you through the convicting power of the Holy Spirit. After conversion, He works in you and ultimately through you. The tragedy is that you refuse to let Him continue "through you." After all, you've been a Christian servant for nearly a hundred days, and now you're to be looked on as a spiritual leader. Surely you can show them, but somehow "the doing of the good" never is realized.

Relax! Take a deep breath! Remember how dependent on God you were in the beginning. Remember how He did the seemingly impossible through you? Did that happen because of you or because of Him? Right! Because of both of you! So why leave Him out now?

Allow God to work in you again, so He can work through you. Then you will both wish and do the good.

Reader's Response

A Prayer to Complete

Lord, I guess I'm guilty of trying to do some things on my own after doing so many things with You. May we together today do . . .

Going Deeper

1. Can you tell from reading Romans 7 what caused Paul to express himself the way he did?
2. Have you had any experience lately similar to the one described where you wanted to do good, but you didn't do it? What were your feelings?
3. What actions could you take that would prevent the above type of experience from happening again?
   (1) _____
   (2) _____
   (3) _____
4. What do you "wish" to do for good today?
5. How can you and God accomplish your "wish" today?

DAY 91 ————————————— DATE ————————

Gains and Losses

"Whatever things were gain to me, those things I have counted as loss for the sake of Christ" (Phil. 3:7).

Christian servant! You have really gained a high level of spirituality! Listen to Paul.

Paul said he was circumcised the eighth day (3:5). This was in fulfillment of God's command (Gen. 17:12; Lev. 12:3). He also said he was "of the nation of Israel" (Phil. 3:5). When Jews wanted to stress their special relationship to God, they used the magic word *Israel.* By being an "Israelite," Paul stressed the absolute purity of his descent.

Further, Paul was "of the tribe of Benjamin" (v. 5). Not only a pure Jew with special relationship to God but of the most aristocratic tribe of Jews. Paul called himself "a Hebrew of the Hebrews" (v. 5). In addition to all the other claims, Paul spoke the fast disappearing, native language of Hebrew.

Paul continued by claiming to be a Pharisee, a spiritual leader of Judaism (v. 5); so zealous that he persecuted the Christians before his own conversion (v. 6); and as to the Law, "blameless" (v. 6).

You think you've gained credentials? Keep listening to Paul. "Whatsoever things were gain to me, those things I have counted as loss for the sake of Christ" (v. 7). Later he wrote, "Not that I have already obtained it, or have already become perfect, but I press on" (v. 12). Like Hosea, the apostle Paul desired to "press on to know the Lord" (Hos. 6:3).

What about your gains? You'd better learn a lesson from Paul. It will be easier than finding out for yourself.

Reader's Response

A Prayer to Complete

Lord, I give up. All that I have gained I counted as loss for Your sake. Help me to press on today as I . . .

Going Deeper

1. What are three things you have "gained" by being a Christian servant during these hundred days?

(1) _____
(2) _____
(3) _____

2. What have you lost by being a Christian servant during these hundred days?

(1) _____
(2) _____
(3) _____

3. What do you still need to lose in order to gain more of Christ (Phil. 3:11)?

(1) _____
(2) _____
(3) _____

4. What is one lesson you could learn from Paul?

5. What do you need to "press on" to today?

DAY 92 ———————————————— DATE _____
Servant or Priest or Both

"It shall be if He calls you, that you shall say, 'Speak, Lord, for Thy servant is listening' " (1 Sam. 3:9).

When Samuel first heard the call of God, he did not understand it (1 Sam. 3:1-14). Not only did God have to repeat it, but the call had to be interpreted for Samuel by the old priest Eli. One of the functions of a priest was to intercede on one's behalf before God and thus help interpret God's will. When Samuel did understand his call, he responded to it quickly.

Does this sound familiar to you? Several months ago you were trying to decide if what you were hearing and feeling about servanthood was God's call or something else. Someone like Eli came into your struggle and helped you interpret your feelings as God's call, and you began a process that reached to this very day. You ought to give thanks to God for the Elis in your life and pray that there will always be a wise old Eli around.

When Eli finally recognized the presence of God in the situation, he instructed Samuel as to the proper response to the call of God. Without Eli, Samuel was in a state of confusion. Not only should you thank God for sending an Eli into your life to help in your discovery, you should now be prepared to become an Eli to someone else.

Others will hear your experiences as you share them. They will be exposed to all the same types of things to which you were exposed, and they, too, will hear voices and have feelings. Someone, maybe you, will be there as God's "priest" to help that person understand and interpret God's call.

So with whom do you identify in this story: the servant, Samuel; the priest, Eli; or both?

Reader's Response

A Prayer to Complete
Lord, when You spoke, I listened, and here I am. Now help me to also listen in as You speak to my friends. If possible, I'd like to be a "priest" to . . .

Going Deeper
1. From the account of this story in 1 Samuel 3:1-14, list reasons why Samuel did not at first understand God's call.
    (1) Verse 1 _____
    (2) Verse 1 _____
    (3) Verse 7 _____
    (4) Verse 7 _____
2. Are there any reasons that you can remember why you did not at first understand God's call to servanthood?
    (1) _____
    (2) _____
    (3) _____

3. In 1 Samuel 3:11-14 what did God call Samuel to do?
4. How does this relate to what God called you to do, or does it relate at all?
5. List three friends for whom you could be an Eli in their struggle with God's call to servanthood.

   (1) _____

   (2) _____

   (3) _____

DAY 93 ————————————— DATE _____

What's that Noise?

"The people could not distinguish the sound of the shout of joy from the sound of the weeping of the people" (Ezra. 3:13).

The beginning of construction on the new Temple was an occasion for mixed expressions. Those who remembered the past and the former Temple wept out loud (Hag. 2:3; Zech. 4:10). Mixed with the weeping was the sound of joyous shouting as some celebrated the newness of the Temple. It was the final ending of the old, the beginning of the new.

Anytime endings and beginnings come together, there are expressions of mixed feelings. You can observe this phenomenon at graduations, weddings, funerals, and other such occasions when the "good old days" and the "future hope" come crashing together in one event.

So it is with this time in your life. Some experiences of service are over. You listened, you waited, you decided, you served, you waited, you ministered, you waited, you listened, you served, you laughed, you cried, you praised, you hurt, you ministered unto and you were ministered unto, and now it's here. The noise you hear may be that of a Christian servant weeping. Then again, it may be persons weeping that your time of service with them was so meaningful. But tomorrow is here. Back to the routine with the making of new friends and the renewing of old.

What's that noise? It is the noise of one becoming like Christ. " 'I am the Alpha and the Omega,' says the Lord God, 'who is and who was and who is to come, the Almighty' " (Rev. 1:8).

Reader's Response

A Prayer to Complete

Thanks, Lord, for the endings and the beginnings of my life. Thanks for being both. Help me today to . . .

Going Deeper

1. What light do the cross references shed on the mixed expressions at the rebuilding of the Temple?
   (1) Haggai 2:3_____
   (2) Zechariah 4:10 _____
2. List two experiences of mixed emotions in your life where an ending and beginning came together.
   (1) _____
   (2) _____
3. What is the most positive thought you can express about the "good old days" of your past servant experiences?
4. What is your greatest hope for the immediate future?
5. How has this experience of service made you more like Christ?

DAY 94 ——————————— DATE ———————————

What Made the Wise Men Wise?

"When they saw the star . . . and saw the Child . . . they fell down and worshiped Him; and . . . presented to Him gifts and

. . . departed for their own country by another way" (Matt. 2:10-11).

Have you ever wondered why the Wise Men were called wise? I'm sure there were good intellectual and spiritual reasons for this description, but in addition to those, there are three reasons referred to by Matthew that are characteristic of wise persons.

In spite of the fact that tradition says these Wise Men were approximately seventy years old, they still dared to follow a star. Chasing stars should never be limited to one age or peer group. Like Don Quixote in *The Man of LaMancha*, these Wise Men chose to follow the star however far or hopeless it may seem, and in so doing they discovered the new hope of humanity.

Discovering the answer to all men's search, these Wise Men "worshiped" and "presented to Him gifts." Gifts are appropriately presented to both kings and babies, but never was so significant a gift presented or allegiance given to a baby/king. Wise indeed is the person who learns to transfer both allegiance and gifts from the search for truth to the Truth.

Having found one worthy of their worship, these Wise Men returned "by another way." No person ever discovers Jesus Christ and returns the same way again. He was embodied newness provided for us a new way of life, and in the security of that newness, the wise man or wise woman continues to search, worship, give, and go.

Reader's Response

A Prayer to Complete

God of newness, create in me both an appreciation of Truth and a desire to wisely share it today as I . . .

Going Deeper

1. How would you define wisdom?

2. Can you think of any "stars" you've followed recently? What was the result?
3. How do you react to the statement: "Wise indeed is the person who learns to transfer both allegiance and gifts from the search for truth to the Truth"?
4. After you discovered Jesus Christ, you too returned "by another way." Describe your other "way."
5. Name one person with whom you could share your search for and discovery of Truth: _____ .

DAY 95 ──────────── DATE _____
What Happened to All that Seed? (1)

"Behold, the sower went out to sow" (Matt. 13:3).

An obscure question comes out of the Old Testament writings of Haggai. The prophet asked, "Is the seed still in the barn?" (Hag. 2:19). Hopefully, your answer would be a negative one. You have sown seed for a hundred days—a barnful and more. The more appropriate question for you is: "What happened to all that seed?"

Jesus shared a parable with His disciples in which He told of four possible results of seed sowing. As a modern-day disciple, you could well apply His parable to your situation.

Some seed which you sowed fell on hard ground (Matt. 13:4). Your seed, regardless of how well prepared you were to sow it, never had a chance. It never penetrated the hard, unbroken soil. This seed made no converts, changed no lives, produced no harvest. Since the seed never entered the heart and mind of the hearer, all hope of a coming harvest was lost.

Who's fault was it that no harvest came of this seed sown? Some of the blame could be yours, but in all probability it is more the fault of the hearer. This seed never had opportunity to produce. It landed on hard soil and eventually blew away

to the birds, for sometimes a "whirlwind and storm is His way"
(Nah. 1:3).

Reader's Response

A Prayer to Complete

Lord, I don't suppose you like hard soil any more than I do,
but it's there just the same. Since I can't judge, help me be a
seed sower, not a soil sampler, today as I . . .

Going Deeper

1. List three examples from your experiences of sowing seed
   on hard ground.
   (1) _____
   (2) _____
   (3) _____
2. Is there anything you could have done differently in these
   three cases?
   (1) _____
   (2) _____
   (3) _____
3. From Matthew 13 see if you can discover why Jesus told
   this parable to His disciples.
4. What do you think is meant by Nahum 1:3, a "whirlwind
   and storm is His way"?
5. What's wrong with being a "soil sampler" rather than a
   "seed sower"?
   (1) _____
   (2) _____
   (3) _____

DAY 96 ———————————— DATE _____
What Happened to All that Seed? (2)

"Behold, the sower went out to sow" (Matt. 13:3).

Some seed fell on hard ground. What happened to all that other seed? Some of the remainder fell on rocky ground (Matt. 13:5-6) according to the parable of Jesus.

Here in this rocky ground your seed found the soil to be shallow and without sufficient depth for roots. Although this soil allowed almost immediate growth due to it's characteristics of being easily moistened and easily warmed, it also provided a short life span due to rapid drying out.

Some of those with whom you've worked were easily swayed by the gospel but just as easily cooled. They had no roots, no maturity, no stability, no endurance. They were superficial.

Likewise, according to the parable, some of your seed fell among thorns (v. 7). This seed was soon choked by the weeds resulting in a small harvest. These really had potential, but the surroundings were too wild and nonconducive to growth and maturity.

Misplaced priorities, peer pressure, and personal desires created for these a climate in which "everyone did what was right in his own eyes" (Judg. 21:25). Without special care, this seed will never reach full potential.

Reader's Response

A Prayer to Complete

Lord, I realize the importance of follow-up for the seed I've sown. Strengthen those today who nurture my sown seed. Especially help . . .

Going Deeper

1. List three examples from your hundred days of service of sowing seed on rocky ground.

(1) _____

(2) _____

(3) _____

2. Is there anything you could have done different in these cases?

   (1) _____

   (2) _____

   (3) _____

3. List three examples from your hundred days of service of sowing seed in thorns.

   (1) _____

   (2) _____

   (3) _____

4. Is there anything you could have done different in these cases?

   (1) _____

   (2) _____

   (3) _____

5. Who needs follow-up from your seed sowing?

   (1) _____

   (2) _____

   (3) _____

   (4) _____

6. Pray for those who will be following up on these.

DAY 97 ———————————— DATE _____

"Behold Happened to All that Seed?(3)

"Behold a sower went out to sow" (Matt. 13:3).

Some seed fell on hard ground. Some fell on rocky soil. Still other seed fell among thorns. But what about the seed still remaining? Some of your seed fell on good ground.

According to the parable, this seed yielded "a crop, some a hundredfold, some sixty, and some thirty" (v. 8). It was the same seed, the same sower, the same field, so what was the difference? The value of this parable is not its lesson about seed or sower but its lesson about soil. The results do not depend totally on the seed sower but on the condition of the recipient.

The soil in this part of the parable was deep and clean and soft, and the seed could penetrate, find nourishment, and grow. An abundant harvest was the result.

Much of the seed you've sown during these hundred days found it's way to recipient soil. Life roots are getting deeper. Growth is occurring. Maturity is approaching. Harvest is near.

And your response? It is mixed. In spite of your best efforts at seed sowing, some of those with whom you worked have only one response: "Harvest is past, summer is ended,/And we are not saved" (Jer. 8:20). To some, in spite of their growing conditions, you can say with Zechariah, "Rejoice greatly . . ./Shout in triumph . . ./Your king is coming to you" (9:9).

Reader's Response

A Prayer to Complete

Father, thank You for the privilege of sowing seed during these hundred days. Like Job, I have "wept for the one whose life is hard" (Job 30:25). Today, I continue to pray for . . .

Going Deeper

1. List three examples from your hundred days of service of sowing seed on good ground.

    (1) _____

    (2) _____

    (3) _____

2. In each case, state why you think the ground was good.

    (1) _____

    (2) _____

    (3) _____

3. What is the current status of each of the above examples?

(1) _____
(2) _____
(3) _____

4. What is your reaction to Jeremiah 8:20?
5. In what ways have you "wept for the one whose life is hard" (Job 30:25)?

DAY 98 ─────────────────── DATE _____

What Happens When the Sower Becomes Soil and Seed?

"He who has ears, let him hear" (Matt. 13:9).

Have you heard the parable of the sower and seed yet? Have you heard all of it? It is possible that the roles can be reversed? Are you sometimes the soil and seed? How have you received the seed shared with you by others? How well have you taken root and grown?

To a large degree your success in receiving is similar to your success in sowing. Obadiah wrote, "As you have done, it will be done to you./Your dealings will return on your own head" (v. 15).

How would you evaluate your growth during these hundred days of service? Have you taken deeper roots, sprouted new growth, spiritually reproduced? Have you taken on elements that need to be evaluated now that your hundred days of service is nearly over? Do old patterns need to be replaced with newly learned ones so that the new will be visible? Indeed, "The time has arrived for pruning the vines" (Song of Sol. 2:12).

Will your soil hold that which it has received? Perhaps you need to move some rocks, pull some weeds, deepen some levels. Growth that began will not automatically continue when transplanted. "Watch yourselves, that you might not lose what we have accomplished, but that you may receive a full reward" (2 John 8).

Take time now to "Be silent before the Lord God!" (Zeph. 1:7). Ask Him to help you continue to grow after a time of pruning.

Reader's Response

A Prayer to Complete

Lord, grant me the discernment necessary to prune the dead and deadly parts of my life, so I can grow to be more like you. I think I need to begin today by . . .

Going Deeper

1. If Obadiah was right in verse 15, what do you anticipate returning "on your own head"?

2. What are two things that need to be pruned from your life?

   (1) _____

   (2) _____

3. What action could you take to accomplish the pruning of the above items?

   (1) _____

   (2) _____

4. What could you do this week to:

   (1) "Move some rocks" _____

   (2) "Pull some weeds" _____

   (3) "Deepen some levels" _____

5. React to the statement: "Growth that began will not automatically continue when transplanted."

6. What can you do to continue the growth that has begun in you?

184

Enough and More

"Go, sell the oil and pay your debt, and . . . live on the rest" (2 Kings 4:7).

In this most interesting and applicable account from the life of Elisha, a widow was about to lose her two sons to pay a dept (2 King 4:1-7). This practice, although strange to us, was common in that day (Ex. 21:7; Lev. 25:39; Neh. 5:5). The widow made appeal to God's prophet for help. Apparently, the answer to her request was limited only by her faith.

Told to collect pots for oil, the widow collected all she could find or perhaps all she really believed God would fill. Then, as instructed, she began to pour what little oil she had into the pots. As long as she poured, there was oil. When there were no more pots to be filled, the oil ceased to flow.

At the beginning of your hundred days of servanthood, you were somewhat unsure of yourself. You wondered if you would have enough spiritual food to feed the hungry, enough spiritual clothing for the naked, enough spiritual medicine for the sick, enough spiritual wisdom for the inquirer. But you learned through faith. The more that was required of you, the more God supplied to you. There was enough.

Notice how the story ends. Elisha said to the widow, "Go, sell the oil and pay your debt, and you and your sons can live on the rest" (2 Kings 4:7). There was enough and more.

You've had enough for your servanthood. You've had it through faith in the God who provides. As you continue there will be more. With God, you can always "live on the rest."

By the way, when the "oil" begins to run low, remember where you got it . . . and how!

Reader's Response

A Prayer to Complete
Father, thanks for continually putting "oil in my lamp" and

supplying all my needs. Thanks also for the "rest." I will need the "rest" now as I . . .

Going Deeper

1. What light do the cross reference Scriptures shed on this account in 2 Kings 4:7?
    (1) Exodus 21:7 _____
    (2) Leviticus 25:39 _____
    (3) Nehemiah 5:5 _____
2. In your opinion, is there any significance that Elisha was not present when the miracle took place?
3. Can you recall four uncertainties you had at the beginning of your hundred days of servanthood?
    (1) _____
    (2) _____
    (3) _____
    (4) _____
4. In what ways did God provide for these uncertainties?
    (1) _____
    (2) _____
    (3) _____
    (4) _____
5. React to the statement: "With God, you can always 'live on the rest.'"
6. What is the "rest" that will carry over into your future service?

DAY 100 ————————— DATE _____
And Now the Future

"Trust in the Lord with all your heart,/And do not lean on your own understanding./In all your ways acknowledge Him,/And He will make your paths straight" (Prov. 3:5-6).

You have learned a secret during these hundred days of service. The secret of finding God's will and receiving His blessing is to trust Him with all your heart and acknowledge Him in all your ways. It is easier, you've learned, to lean upon His understanding rather than your own. You've discovered that one does not plan one's own ways and then ask God to cooperate, but, rather, one acknowledges God and allows Him to make the way straight and clear.

In "all" areas of life God is to be acknowledged. Thoughts of Him are not to be limited to specific assignments or sacred places. He is to be acknowledged where you live, work, study, and play. He is not an elective. He is a requirement.

Acknowledging Him requires recognition of who He is and who you are. "It is He who has made us, and not we ourselves" (Ps. 100:3). Upon Him we are to depend for everything.

So this much you have learned and more: God is the source of all; He has made you to be dependent on Him; you are to live in a consciousness of that dependence; God will provide all you need; you are to trust Him and acknowledge Him in all.

An ant and an elephant crossed an old wooden bridge together one day. As they walked, the bridge rattled and squeaked while the weight moved it back and forth. The bridge gave every indication that the weight was too much for it to hold up under. When, finally, the two had crossed the still-swaying bridge, the ant turned to the elephant and exclaimed, "Man, we really shook that thing, didn't we!"

Give credit where credit is due, and walk on in that acknowledgment.

Reader's Response

A Prayer to Complete
Thank you, Lord, for my servant experiences. We really shook it, didn't we! I acknowledge Your presence in my life and trust Your leadership as I . . .

Going Deeper
1. What are three areas of concern related to your future?
   (1) _____
   (2) _____
   (3) _____
2. How can you trust God with each of these areas?
   (1) _____
   (2) _____
   (3) _____
3. What are some ways you can give God the credit for your experiences of the past hundred days?
   (1) _____
   (2) _____
   (3) _____
   (4) _____
   (5) _____
4. What do you think the writer of Proverbs meant by: "He will make your paths straight" (Prov. 3:6)?
5. You have written many thoughts in this book. Who could you share these thoughts with in the next few weeks—a friend, a minister, a family member? Determine now to share your thoughts with someone soon.

Conclusion

After taking all one hundred pills in my prescription, I went back to the doctor for an evaluation. I had mixed feelings. While on the one hand, I wanted to be relieved of the discipline of taking a pill each day, on the other hand, I wanted to continue to be as healthy as I had been over the past three months. I was not surprised to hear my doctor say, "We've got a good thing going; let's stay with it."

After a hundred days of singular servanthood, I hope you

have a good thing going and that you have already committed yourself to continue. There are numerous books that will assist you in a daily pattern of reading. You may also want to begin reading through the Bible. Several systematic plans are available to assist you to read through the Bible in one year. Whatever your strategy, I challenge you to continue in the assurance that "he who began a good work in you will carry it on to completion" (Phil. 1:6, NIV).

APPENDIXES

Appendix A
Acknowledgments

The seeds of this book were sown in my interaction with student summer missionaries who taught me that daily service apart from daily worship equals spiritual burnout. As their student director/minister, I wrote letters, designed Bible studies, sent weekly memos, made cassette tapes and did a dozen other things to try to keep them "up" spiritually during their term of service.

Ten years after working with my first student summer missionary, these seed ideas were transplanted to the hotbed of a seminary doctoral program. The result was a Doctor of Ministry project at Southwestern Baptist Seminary in Fort Worth, Texas, entitled, *Developing a Program of Private Worship for Student Short-Term Missionaries.*

Five more years of interacting with short-term missionaries further cultivated this material resulting in *First Things First: A Daily Guide for Summer Missionaries* printed by the Southern Baptist Home Mission Board and distributed to thousands of student summer missionaries.

Finally, these materials were refined and broadened in scope and perspective and have now taken the form of this book, hopefully addressing the needs of individuals who commit themselves to Christian servanthood.

The following persons served as student summer missionaries related to my ministry and as such made their contributions to the development of the materials in this book. My thanks to the following summer servants (realizing that many of the females will have new last names since my last contact with them). Their places of service are listed in parentheses.

From Pan American University, Willie Almanza (Oregon), Carolyn Archer (Indiana), Tura Hatley Cason (Texas), Don Egle (Wisconsin), Mickey Ewing (Texas), Donald Fields (California), Nati Garza (Oregon), Janie Gonzales (California), Oralia Gonzalez (Utah), Brenda Hale (Texas), Wayne Hein (New York), Jan Houston (Missouri), Penny McCormick (Missouri), Jesse Palomo (Puerto Rico), Elias Pantoja (Texas), Tony Sanchez (Mexico), Chris Cathey Shuford (Ohio), Janie Sigle (Oregon), Evelyn Simmons (Virginia), Susan Snowden (Indiana), Janet Stowe (Texas), Sue Ellen Wicks (Texas), and Jenny Wilks (Texas).

From East Texas State University, Janet Powell Adams (Michigan), Joyce Ashcraft (Texas), Doug Bench (Virginia), Cheryl Bradley (South Carolina), Ann Cantrell (North Carolina), Ronnie Conyers (Pennsylvania), Cindi Moore Coss (Washington DC), Steve Culpepper (Michigan), Cynthia Dement Cunnyngham (Texas; Eastern Europe), Hal Cunnyngham (Bangladesh), Debbie Darr (Ohio), Nancy Mizell Davis (New York), Ferrell Foster (Texas), Tommy Glenn (California), Joe Gilbert (Georgia), Charlotte Strawn

Glover (Arizona; Florida), Wade Glover (Florida; New York), Garvon Golden (Texas), Carol Palmore Gonzalez (Texas), Richard Harrison (Canada), Glenda Haywood (Tennessee), Robert Hood (Texas), Deb Miller Horan (Texas), Annet Lamb Hyde (Texas), Sheila Moser Ingle (Arizona), Jolene Belt Jackson (Texas), Sharon Jackson (Washington), Webb Jones (Tennessee), Mary Latimer (Arizona), David Mabe (New York), Vanita Martin (Pennsylvania), Dena Johnson Moran (Texas; Kentucky), Martha Morris (Pennsylvania), Steve Nevins (Texas), Lydia Ochoa (Pennsylvania; Texas), Carolyn McCreary Ramsey (Arizona), Dianne Ward Ross (Texas), Ronny Ross (Canada; California), Kathy Stone (Texas), Peggy Travis (Texas), Penny Travis (Texas), and Linda Wright (New Mexico).

From the University of Texas, Sue Adams (Pennsylvania), Susan Aiken (Georgia), Steve Arnold (Texas), Pam Ballard (Florida), Eddie Barker (Maryland), Debbie Barron (Maine), Teresa Batey (California; Missouri), Danny Blackmon (Louisiana), David Brewer (Idaho; Washington), Mike Burson (Arizona), Retta Cammack (Alabama), David Campbell (Scotland), Kin Cheng (California), Tommy Chiodo (Georgia), Bill Clark (New York), Tom Collier (Texas), Becky Colvin (Pennsylvania), Mark Dawson (Texas), Bill Dean (Texas), Martha DeLuna (California), Dennis Doyle (California; Utah), Karen Morris Doyle (Texas), Becky Finley (Wyoming), Lorena Foard (Texas), Kim Forehand (Canada), Elva Garza (Mexico), Kelley Green (Missouri), Carolyn Greenfield (Texas), Gayle Brown Gresson (New York), J. J. Griffin (Nebraska), Ewin Groce (Texas), Paul Gustafson (Delaware), Vicki Heath (Washington/Oregon), John Hille (Tennessee), Gary Holley (Washington/Oregon), Carl Hoover (Brazil), Dona Hopkins (California), Richard Jeffus (Tennessee), La Jolly (California), Kathy Lawton Kirk (Florida), Sharon Long (Virginia), Thomas Mantooth (Minnesota/Wisconsin), Brenda Colvin Marsh (Missouri), Sharon Leftwich Miller (Iowa), Pam Dowies Owens (Texas; Guadalupe), Randy Owens (Canada), Mark Perkins (Texas), June Porter (Texas), Walt Reep (Vermont), Pam Sawyer (Texas), Donna Shackelford (Wisconsin), Kelly Moore Westenhouver (Texas), Pat Wilkendorf (Texas), and Beverly Williams (Texas).

As a part of the Doctor of Ministry project, four persons were extremely helpful. My thanks to Drs. Charles Ashby, Jimmy Nelson, Rick Spencer, and Browning Ware for their contributions to the development of the materials in this book.

Thanks are also in order to numerous single servants who, in seminars and workshops, have helped broaden the scope and perspective of these materials.

A special thanks to Jan Duke for her hours of manuscript typing, serving in the shadows, yet, nonetheless, serving.

And to all those who faithfully supported the idea through the years of its seeding, cultivation, and growth, thanks. To whatever degree I have served my God, it is a direct result of faithful Christians who have been God's servants in my life. I feel a special thanks to all of those who have served outside the spotlight, without fanfare and largely without acknowledgment. Their faithful-servant support has encouraged me to be more of the servant God wants me to be.

> God doth not need
> Either man's work, or His own gifts; who best
> Bear His mild yoke, they serve Him best: His state
> Is kingly; thousands at His bidding speed,
> And post o'er land and ocean without rest;
> They also serve who only stand and wait.[1]

1. John Milton, "Sonnet on His Blindness," *One Hundred and One Famous Poems* (Chicago: Contemporary Books, Inc., 1958), p. 91.

Appendix B
Index of Scripture References

\